insight text guide

Adam Kealley

Bad Dreams and Other Stories

Tessa Hadley

First published in 2022, reprinted in 2024, 2025.

Insight Publications Pty Ltd
3/350 Charman Road
Cheltenham VIC 3192
Australia
Tel: +61 3 8571 4950
Email: books@insightpublications.com.au

www.insightpublications.com.au

A catalogue record for this book is available from the National Library of Australia

Tessa Hadley's Bad Dreams and Other Stories / Adam Kealley

Adam Kealley asserts the moral right to be identified as the author of this work.

ISBNs:
9781922771087 (print)
9781922771094 (digital)

Cover design by Melisa Paredes

Printed by Markono Print Media Pte Ltd

contents

STORY TABLE

Title	Perspective	Protagonist	Other significant characters	Central Event
An Abduction	Third person omniscient	Jane Allsop	Daniel, Nigel, Paddy and Fiona	Jane is picked up by the three boys and sleeps with Daniel.
The Stain	Third person omniscient	Marina	The old man, Wendy, Anthony, Gary, Liam	Marina, the old man's housekeeper, is left his house in his will.
Deeds Not Words	Third person limited	Edith Carew	Laura Mulhouse, Fitzsimmon Briers	Edith has an affair with fellow teacher Fitzsimmon, which ends when World War I begins.
One Saturday Morning	Third person limited	Carrie	Dom Smith, Carrie's mother	Dom Smith arrives at Carrie's house unexpectedly, on the day of a dinner party.
Experience	First person	Laura	Hana, Julian	Laura moves into Hana's house and attempts to seduce Julian, Hana's ex-lover.
Bad Dreams	Shifting third person limited	An unnamed young girl	The girl's mother and father	The young girl overturns the furniture in the living room.
Flight	Third person limited	Claire	Susan, Amy, Ben, Ryan	On a business trip, Claire visits her estranged sister, Susan, whose daughter Amy has had a baby.
Under the Sign of the Moon	Third person limited	Greta	Mitchell, Kate, Ian, Graham, Boyd	On the train to visit her daughter, Greta meets Mitchell, who invites her to a second meeting.
Her Share of Sorrow	Third person omniscient	Ruby	Dalia, Adrian, Nico	On holiday, Ruby falls in love with classic books and decides to write her own novel.
Silk Brocade	Shifting third person limited	Ann Gallagher	Kit Seaton, Nola Higgins, Ray, Donny Ross, Blaise Perney, Sally Ross	Nola asks Ann to make her wedding dress, then passes away suddenly. Later, Sally visits Nola's home.

OVERVIEW

About the author

A writer of novels, short stories and nonfiction, Tessa Hadley (née Nichols) was born in Bristol, UK in 1956. Her father was a teacher and jazz musician, her mother an artist and dressmaker. Hadley, a passionate reader, came to writing success later in her life, having trained as a teacher following an English degree at Cambridge University. Leaving the profession after only a year, she married and had three sons in addition to raising three stepsons. In her thirties, Hadley enrolled in an MA in Creative Writing at Bath Spa University, before completing a PhD on the writer Henry James, an experience that she credits with giving her the confidence to write authoritatively in her own style. Her first novel, *Accidents in the Home*, was published when Hadley was forty-six.

Hadley has published several novels, including *Accidents in the Home* (2002), *The Master Bedroom* (2007) and *Free Love* (2022), as well as short-story collections. With her husband Eric Hadley she has also published two collections of creation myths from around the world: *Legends of the Sun and Moon* (1983) and *Legends of Earth, Air, Fire and Water* (1985). Her stories, as well as extracts from her novels, have also been published in journals such as *The New Yorker* and *Granta*. Her PhD thesis resulted in a nonfiction book: *Henry James and the Imagination of Pleasure* (2002).

Her narratives are realist in style and set in England between the early twentieth century and the present day. They typically examine the experiences of women, often in terms of the psychological ramifications of family relationships, sexual encounters, or seemingly innocuous events. Her stories observe rich details within ordinary lives.

Hadley has twice won the O. Henry Prize for short stories (for 'The Card Trick' in 2005 and 'Valentine' in 2014), as well as the Windham-Campbell Literature Prize for fiction (2016) and the Edge Hill Short Story

Prize (for *Bad Dreams* in 2018). She has also been long- and short-listed for several other awards. She was elected a Fellow of the Royal Society of Literature in 2009 and is also a Fellow of The Welsh Academy. Hadley lives in Cardiff, Wales, and was until recently a Professor of Creative Writing at Bath Spa University.

Synopsis

Bad Dreams contains ten stories, all set in England and with temporal settings ranging from around 1914 to the present day. Each story centres on female protagonists, both women and young girls, reflecting on the potency of personal experience. In many of the stories, conflict derives from the protagonist crossing the threshold from innocence to experience, often with the transformation of the ordinary into something deeply and psychologically significant. Such transitions can be unforeseen – a chance meeting with a stranger, an unexpected visitor – while others are actively courted by the protagonist. In several stories, Hadley manipulates perspective and chronology, allowing events to be observed from multiple angles and distances, and illuminating the unanticipated consequences of events in the characters' lives.

In many of the stories there is an undercurrent of desire. Characters are driven by a sense of alienation or dissatisfaction, with a concomitant yearning for connection or experience. Hadley explores the tensions arising from the satisfaction of such desires, whereby exhilaration is often tempered by disillusionment. In doing so, she creates stories that reveal the vulnerabilities of the characters and the burden of inexperience. All of the stories, however, reveal the resilience of their female protagonists. Despite the disappointments and heartbreaks, there are realisations of personal growth and even triumph arising from the knowledge gained about the world, and, importantly, about the self. While such moments may be oblique, they are nevertheless present, leading to a collection that explores the bittersweet nature of change.

BACKGROUND & CONTEXT

Publication and production history

Most of the short stories in this collection have been published previously, including in *The New Yorker, The Atlantic* and *The Guardian Weekend Magazine*. It is common for short stories initially to be published in literary journals and magazines; although the stories in *Bad Dreams* are published as a single volume – which can be discussed in terms of common themes, ideas and even character types – each story does stand alone, and they were composed independently and at different times. This might influence the way you analyse and discuss the collection as a whole.

Identifying the connections between the stories does suggest Hadley's interest in women's experience, but considering the differences can be enlightening too. For example, 'Experience' is the only story written in first person. Other differences of note include the decision to leave the characters in 'Bad Dreams' unnamed, and that 'The Stain' explores the relationship between a housekeeper and her employer, a different kind of intimate relationship from the lovers and families that concern most of the other stories. Such differences can provide you with useful points of focus for your exploration and discussion.

Settings

The stories in this collection are set in England, some within cities and others within small rural or coastal towns. The cities tend to be named – 'Under the Sign of the Moon' is set largely in Liverpool and 'Flight' in Leeds, for example – while the smaller towns are simply identified as a village or town in a specific location (such as Surrey in 'An Abduction'), or simply a village ('The Stain'). Most take place within familiar domestic settings, and Hadley creates a strong sense of such places through the careful selection of detail. Consider:

- descriptions of the protagonists' homes in 'One Saturday Morning' and 'Bad Dreams', both viewed through the eyes of children
- descriptions of others' homes in 'An Abduction', 'The Stain', 'Experience' or 'Silk Brocade', and how other characters' intimate spaces are depicted through the eyes of the visiting protagonist
- descriptions of places that were once home, such as Greta's recollection of Liverpool in 'Under the Sign of the Moon' or Claire's return to the family home in 'Flight'.

As you read, note contextual clues that help establish geographical settings and locations. Furthermore, note how Hadley creates an atmosphere of disorientation or estrangement, even within places that were once familiar to the characters, through the inclusion of unsettling details. Start to draw connections between the depictions of these familiar or intimate spaces and the themes and ideas Hadley explores.

Historical and social contexts

The stories explore a range of historical and social contexts, often significant in underscoring key themes of the story. The earliest is 'Deeds Not Words', which is set just prior to the outbreak of World War I and within the context of the radical political action of the Women's Social and Political Union (WSPU). Edith's affair with Fitzsimmon is interrupted by his enrolment in the military, and her subsequent heartache and shame are correlated with those of her suffragist colleague, Laura. 'The Stain', although set in contemporary times, recalls colonial South African racial politics to explore the complex relationship between Marina and her employer, an émigré and former member of the South African Defence Force, who was implicated in an undisclosed atrocity. In these cases, the historical settings help contrast the individual experience of a character with wider social attitudes regarding women and their roles.

Other stories encompass significant time spans, such as 'An Abduction', which begins in the 1960s but concludes with its now-grown protagonist speaking to a counsellor forty years later. In 'Under the Sign of the Moon', Greta recollects her first marriage to Ian in the

1970s, when she lived an unconventional lifestyle, which contrasts sharply with the apparent conservatism of both her second marriage and her daughter's relationship with Boyd. Such shifts in time allow the experiences of the central character to be reviewed from another perspective grounded in a different social context.

Those stories set in more recent times are less specific in their temporality. In 'Flight', Hadley references Facebook, mobile phones, and outdated 1980s furniture, while in 'Under the Sign of the Moon', contemporary environmental consciousness is evident in Boyd's careful recycling and Mitchell's concerns over air travel. Such generalisable details locate the stories in the present without the risk of being dated through specific references. The various historical and social settings in the book highlight both commonalities and differences in the experiences of women, and their understanding of the world around them.

Personal context

A number of the stories in *Bad Dreams* stem from Hadley's own experiences. In a 2013 conversation with Deborah Treisman for *The New Yorker*, she revealed that the nightmare in 'Bad Dreams' was a childhood experience of hers, and that she has been haunted by the phrase *'a ripe old age'* (p.116) ever since, horrified at the glimpse into an adult world that the nightmare offered. Similarly, she also upturned the furniture, in an 'odd impulse to take power, to intervene in [her] parents' adult world' (Treisman 2013). The description of the house in 'One Saturday Morning' is that of her own childhood home, with the experience of inspecting her mother's dressing table manifesting 'the ghost of her future self' (Treisman 2014). The mother's act of giving up art school (in 'Bad Dreams'), overawed by the returned servicemen who were mature-aged students, is drawn from Hadley's own mother's experience, and she 'borrowed fragments of [her] mother's history' for Ann, in 'Silk Brocade' (Treisman 2015). Praised for her psychological insight, Hadley's skill in writing about women's lives derives from a lifetime of reflecting on her own formative experiences.

GENRE, STRUCTURE & LANGUAGE

Realism

Hadley's stories fit within the realism genre, perhaps unsurprising when she counts the realist writer Henry James as shaping her own style. Realism strives for an unembellished depiction of life, often with a keen eye on the tension between the individual and the society that shapes their existence. With its rich but often prosaic language, and focus on characters in familiar, recognisable settings, *Bad Dreams* offers readers a realistic examination of the everyday anxieties afflicting those characters. The realities explored here are typically domestic, leading Claire Hanson to characterise Hadley's oeuvre as belonging to the neodomestic subgenre of realism (Hanson 2015). Some stories seem drawn from Hadley's own experiences, such as Ruby's desire to write, driven by Hadley's 'urge to capture what is actual around [her]' (Kellaway 2022). The subject matter of each story tends towards experiences that may seem commonplace: a childhood discovery, an affair, family relationships, a bad dream. However, in Hadley's hands these events are revealed to be unexpectedly powerful and intriguing.

To say Hadley's prose is largely unadorned is not to say her writing is banal. The complexity in her style tends to come from the juxtaposition of the everyday with the unexpected or uncanny, which Claire Jarvis has described as 'a perplexing, but compelling, blend of familiarity and idiosyncrasy' undercut by 'something gently malign' (Jarvis 2017). Details are nuanced and richly observed, such as the depiction of Carrie practising the piano in 'One Saturday Morning' while anxious over a misplaced and crudely sexual letter she has written to a friend, or the way in which the decor is suddenly critiqued by the intrusion of a narrative voice that remarks that today it looks 'rickety, amateurish' (p.71). Further richness comes from the subtle observations of human behaviour and relationships, such as Jane's sudden insight into the power dynamics between Daniel and his friends in 'An Abduction'. While Hadley's writing is not devoid of symbolism or figurative devices, it is more notable for its finely tuned sense of detail and psychological insight.

The suburban gothic

Many of Hadley's stories contain elements of the suburban gothic genre. In fact, Hadley herself has commented on the haunted quality of her writing (Niedenthal 2017). Although originating in anxieties regarding the suburban development of the United States in the 1950s, the genre spread to other suburban cultures throughout the late twentieth century. The suburban gothic is characterised by an adaptation of traditional gothic tropes, such as the imprisoned heroine, the haunted house, the doppelganger and the return of the repressed into a claustrophobic suburban context. The genre reflects the anxieties and fears of the middle classes regarding insularity, consumerism, conformity and loss of individual identity, exacerbated by the typically monocultural nature of middle-class suburban communities. Paranoia around the safety of women and children is a thematic concern within the genre, too, as well as a recognition that the twentieth-century villain was rarely an externalisable monster but often a neighbour who seemed just like everyone else. This results in a disquieting sense of fear in a setting that appears, on the surface, to be aesthetic, ordered and safe.

Hadley's stories collectively address anxieties of a number of middle-class female characters. 'An Abduction' is clearly gothic in this way; a young woman is ostensibly abducted and exploited while her parents do not even notice. The houses in 'The Stain' and 'Her Share of Sorrow', and even the converted school in 'Deeds Not Words', recall grand gothic manors, home to secrets and transgressions. 'One Saturday Morning' and 'Bad Dreams' both feature comfortable middle-class suburban homes made suddenly uncanny and unsettling for their occupants. Descriptive details, such as the rabbit droppings in the children's teacups in 'An Abduction', the rotting stoat Marina discovers in 'The Stain', or the nasogastric force-feeding of suffragettes in 'Deeds Not Words', also point symbolically to the corruption within these seemingly benign middle-class communities. Other gothic features include Hadley's use of shifting points of view, or shifts in time, which offer an uncanny double perspective on the events of the story, as well as a concern with the psychological condition of her protagonists.

The short-story form

Although it may seem obvious, it is also worthwhile recognising that *Bad Dreams* is a collection of short stories. Short stories tend to be defined as individual works of fiction between 1000 and 15 000 words. They are typically – although not always – concerned with only a few characters, a single event and a limited range of settings. What is important to consider is how Hadley experiments with the short-story form, for example by introducing shifting perspectives, as in 'Bad Dreams' or 'Silk Brocade', or including startling leaps forward in time, as in 'An Abduction' and 'Silk Brocade'. Hadley's manipulation of the short-story form in this way invites readers to look again at the central events, suddenly conscious of new perceptions or implications.

Another consideration is Hadley's construction of plot. Somewhat unusually for short stories, plots in *Bad Dreams* can seem somewhat indistinct. Hadley herself has said that plot 'is the hardest thing to get right' and her advice to students is to 'just dream it' (Kellaway 2022). Many of her stories have a meandering, dreamlike quality. 'One Saturday Morning' is an example, as the story traverses Carrie's piano practice, the arrival of Dom and the eventual news of his wife's death, his attendance at the party during which he makes a pass at Carrie's mother, and finishes with an intimate moment between the mother and her two children. While the events are chronologically sequenced, the focus is on Carrie's negotiation of what she observes, and her naive perspective on adult grief and sexuality. Other stories parallel seemingly disparate narratives, such as in 'Silk Brocade', where Nola's death before her wedding dress could be made is paired with Sally's loss of the jacket subsequently constructed from its fabric. The reader is left to draw connections between these two women's experiences without Hadley drawing a direct causal link between the events.

Structure of individual stories

In each story, the protagonist faces a conflict that shifts them from a degree of innocence or inexperience to a maturity that is sometimes painful. The pace in getting to such conflicts has been described as sometimes 'leisurely' (Cutaia 2017), as Hadley spends time on seemingly innocuous details that nevertheless set the context in which the character develops. Conflicts are often more complex than they initially seem. Carrie's awareness of Dom's grief in 'One Saturday Morning' is complicated by the pass he makes at her mother and Carrie's surprising insight that he is driven by a desire for consolation. In 'An Abduction', Jane's sexual awakening is followed soon after by rejection as Daniel spends much of the night with Fiona – the true significance of which is revealed only later, when Jane is in therapy, and the reader understands both the long-term ramifications of this event and the therapist's casually dismissive attitude that minimises Jane's experience.

Another structural feature is that the protagonists are often paralleled with other women, or other incarnations of themselves, who act as a kind of foil. Jane in 'An Abduction', for example, is contrasted with the more worldly Fiona, and later with her middle-aged self, while Laura in 'Experience' is juxtaposed with the more worldly Hana. In 'Under the Sign of the Moon', Greta's recollection of her unconventional first marriage stands in stark contrast with her second and suggests a motivation in meeting up with Mitchell while in Liverpool. Hadley uses these foils to different effect in each story, but it is through their contrast that the experience of the protagonist is brought into sharp focus.

The endings of stories can vary considerably. Hadley has said that endings are extremely important, as the process of reading a short story means we are held in suspension until the ending, after which the story 'rearranges itself retrospectively' (Hall and Hadley 2017). Thus in analysing *Bad Dreams*, it is useful to consider the implications generated by each story's ending. Several end with a shift in perspective, either to a different character or to a different point in time. 'An Abduction' is an example of this: the story suddenly moves forward in time by forty years, contrasting Jane's desire to return to that transgressive moment she shared with Daniel (despite her discovery of him in bed with Fiona) with the fact that Daniel has completely forgotten about Jane in his own adult life. Similarly, in 'Bad Dreams', the narrative shifts from the daughter to the mother.

Other endings find the central character grasping for a degree of control over their lives, such as in 'The Stain,' in which Marina refuses the bequest of the old man's house, despite the financial security it might bring, refusing to compromise her integrity. Some endings are more oblique, concluding with the shaming of the protagonist for their desires. For example, Greta in 'Under the Sign of the Moon' is left confused and embarrassed at Mitchell's sudden and inappropriate intimacy; Ruby, in 'Her Share of Sorrow', embarrassed at the naivety of her writing being made public, viciously kills off her characters. The endings of the stories range from concrete to ambiguous, the latter perhaps reflecting Hadley's observation about the freedom of the short-story form: 'you can throw out ideas irresponsibly, without needing to ever see them through' (Smart 2020). *Bad Dreams* illustrates women's experiences, and the parallels between their intimate lives and the societies that shape them, while often leaving the reader to draw their own conclusions.

Structure of the collection

An important structural element in a collection of short stories is the order in which stories are presented. In *Bad Dreams,* the collection begins and ends with stories that contrast the experiences of young women with their adult counterparts. 'An Abduction' focuses on Jane's adolescent experience – her sexual awakening with Daniel – and its impact on her adult sense of self, as she haltingly tries to explain the significance of this event to her therapist. 'Silk Brocade' begins with Ann's experience in the past as she reconnects with Nola and, at Thwaite Park, begins a relationship with Donny Ross. It finishes, however, with one of Hadley's characteristic jumps to the present, as Sally – Ann and Donny's daughter – finds herself engaging in intimacy with a boy at Thwaite Park. In opening and closing the collection with these two stories, the editors encourage readers to focus on the interactions between past and present, appropriate for a collection in which the settings encompass a century.

In between these two stories, the rest of the collection alternates between contemporary and historical settings, and child and adult protagonists. What connects them are the experiences of women as they traverse the boundary between some form of inexperience to new knowledge or understanding. In doing so, Hadley encourages readers to see that, despite shifting contexts, the past continues to haunt the present and adult knowledge is formed through lived experience.

The women in the collection are often unsettled by the actions of others, whether they be men (the exploitative Daniel in 'An Abduction') or other women (Hana is disconcerted by Laura's spending time with Julian, Hana's ex-lover, in 'Experience'), even when those actions are misinterpreted (such as the mother's assumptions about her husband in 'Bad Dreams'). Whether such experience and the self-awareness it brings empowers or disempowers the protagonists often remains ambiguous, but nevertheless the impacts remain significant in shaping their psychology, and all the more so for being noticed, if only by the protagonist themselves.

Language

While her stories are rich and descriptive, Hadley's use of language is frequently prosaic rather than lyrical. It has been described as having a 'supple, non-attention-seeking articulacy' (Kellaway 2022), relying on carefully selected detail and fluidity in its syntax rather than on figurative devices. Alex Clark (2011) suggests Hadley 'veers away from the jaw-dropping finale or the linguistic pyrotechnics towards unshowy description and the gradual but ambiguous revelation of character and circumstance'.

Hadley's stories are concise, the longest only thirty pages, suggesting her efficiency with language. There are, however, frequent moments of rich descriptive detail. The 'rotting head of some creature caught in the cleft branch of a tree' (p.52) in 'The Stain' is elaborated upon in gruesome detail; the sexual tension between Ann and Donny is described as 'like a sparking, dangerous live wire' as they lie 'in the long grass under a tall ginkgo tree, whose leaves were shaped like exquisite tiny paddles, translucent bright grass-green' (pp.210–11). This has the effect of slowing the pace, creating strong sensory imagery, and directing the reader's attention to seemingly innocuous details that actually have later significance.

Often such descriptive detail is built around domestic settings, with acutely rendered depictions of the spaces women occupy. Characteristic of neodomestic realism, many of the settings are family homes, with furniture, utensils and ornaments described in detail, such as the living room in 'Bad Dreams' or the mother's dressing table in 'One Saturday Morning'. Undercutting this vivid description, however, are uncanny details that unsettle the reader. For example, in 'Bad Dreams' the wrought-iron light fitting seems 'suddenly as barbaric as a cage or a portcullis in a castle' (p.117) while the goatskin rug had 'half reverted to its animal past' (p.118), unnerving the young protagonist. In revealing a dark undercurrent to everyday domestic settings, Hadley points to the hidden emotional violence that can permeate suburbia and the family home.

Hadley's dialogue is presented without quotation marks, instead introduced by dashes, which gives it an air of distance, as if it is indirectly reported to us. This adds to the observational quality of her stories, preventing us from being fully immersed in the immediacy of action and dialogue. Hadley also makes use of asides to comment on the character or scene, reminding readers of the observational nature of these stories. For example, Jane in 'An Abduction' is described in parentheses as not being 'clever or literary' and as 'nervous of new words' (p.1). Similarly, the narrator's comment that the decor in 'One Saturday Morning' would 'look unexpectedly austere ... amateurish' today (p.70) serves to create narrative distance, reminding readers that just as we are looking back on the events of these stories, we are also looking back on earlier cultural understandings around gender that they represent.

Intertextual references

Hadley frequently references other literary works, including Dante Gabriel Rossetti in 'Deeds Not Words', Arthur Ransome's *Swallows and Amazons* in 'Bad Dreams' and sensation fiction in 'Her Share of Sorrow'. Such references underscore themes in Hadley's own writing, such as the quote from Keats in 'An Abduction' that 'heard melodies are sweet, but those unheard are sweeter' (p.23), reflecting the rich meanings to be found under the surface in this collection of 'everyday' women and girls. Similarly, the quote from Rossetti recalled by Edith, '*I have been here before, / But when or how I cannot tell*' (p.57) points to the interlacing of these women's experiences across the various historical time periods of their settings.

The frequent reference to literary texts also adds a metafictional aspect to the collection. In drawing attention to her characters' fascination with literature, Hadley draws attention to the reader's own relationship with *Bad Dreams*. Claire Jarvis (2017) suggests there is a degree of schadenfreude (deriving pleasure from someone else's misfortune) in reading stories such as Hadley's, noting that 'readers are often dissatisfied with happy endings, vastly preferring the ambivalent or downright bad' (Jarvis 2017). Hadley's intertextual references, along with the observational tone, position the reader as voyeur, savouring the details of these women's experiences.

Symbolism

Hadley's stories frequently contain complex symbolism. In 'Experience', for example, the attic key unlocks Laura's awareness of a world of desire and sensuality that has hitherto been repressed. However, the outlandish style of the key, 'like something in a novel or a pantomime' (p.90), suggests the performative nature of Laura's attempts to emulate Hana by seducing Julian. The grand house in 'The Stain' stands for 'the grandeur and beauty' (p.32) of the privileged life unfamiliar to the working-class Marina. However, the 'dingy' interior (p.32) creates a disjunct between perception and reality, as Marina discovers the grubbiness of the old man and his family: his suspicious past with the South African Defence Force, his inappropriate overtures to Marina, the greediness of his family. The title, too, is symbolic, the idea of a stain prefacing Marina's understanding that 'you couldn't undo the knowledge' (p.52) after confronting unpleasant realities.

Other significant symbols include:

- the discarded Jokari set that could symbolise the loss of Jane's childhood innocence ('An Abduction')
- the dead creature Marina once found in the forest, symbolic of unexpected confrontations with grim realities ('The Stain')
- Laura's force-feeding, symbolising how patriarchal society disciplines female behaviour considered transgressive ('Deeds Not Words')
- the fascinating yet strangely lascivious insect that lands on the children's book, representative of Carrie's unsettling and unexpected encounter with adult themes ('One Saturday Morning')

- the epilogue to *Swallows and Amazons* created in the child's nightmare, symbolising the way in which women are disciplined into normative gender roles ('Bad Dreams')
- the layers of history evident in the train cutting in, symbolic of the layers of experience forming Greta's identity, as well as the dilapidated glasshouse filled with flourishing tropical plants, which represents the tension between Greta's weakened body and her repressed desire ('Under the Sign of the Moon').

Particularly powerful symbolism also belongs to the collection's title, *Bad Dreams*, suggestive of the various nightmares, or simply unfulfilled dreams, that characterise the experiences of the women in these stories.

STORY-BY-STORY ANALYSIS

An Abduction (pp.1–29)

Summary: *Fifteen-year-old Jane accepts an invitation to accompany Daniel, Paddy and Nigel in their car. They return to Nigel's house, where they find Fiona, Nigel's sister. After swimming in the pool, Jane loses her virginity to Daniel. The next morning, she wakes to find Daniel in bed with Fiona. Disappointed, Jane returns home. Years later, she recounts the incident to her therapist.*

This first story establishes themes that recur throughout the collection. It charts Jane's journey from innocence and a desire for experience to adult knowledge, a journey that for her has lasting implications.

Jane is a young woman on the cusp of adulthood. No longer a child like her younger sister, she is frustrated at her liminal condition and feels she should have 'more thoroughly embarked on her teenage self' (p.3), like those schoolmates 'ahead of her in the fated trek towards adulthood' (p.4). The Jokari set – a ball attached to an elastic band designed to be hit with a paddle – becomes a symbol of her situation, as she yearns to be free but remains tethered to her childhood. When the boys first see her, the image presented is one of contradictions, childish yet 'not a child either', in which something 'that was normally hidden' is revealed (p.8): a nascent sexuality and hunger for experience.

Observing the older characters triggers an adult insight that comes 'all at once' (p.13). Jane understands the power Daniel holds not only over her, but also over the other boys, with his worldliness. She recognises in Fiona's flirtation with Daniel the competition that can exist between women, accepting her 'defeat' by the 'older, prettier, more sophisticated girl' (p.17). Daniel, though, recognises something 'raw' in Jane, in contrast to Fiona's affectations. Their ensuing sexual act is 'clumsy' but Jane longs to repeat the experience (p.24). Finding Daniel in bed with Fiona the next morning, Jane is devastated but nevertheless retains control of her emotions, putting up a barrier that persists throughout her adult life. Upon returning home, the setting seems uncanny, 'as if she'd never seen the place before' (p.26). The discarded Jokari set transforms into a symbol of childhood left behind, and her ensuing painful menstruation suggests her awakening to adult sexuality, her first formative experience tainted by Daniel's faithlessness.

The ending of the story jumps forty years ahead. Jane, now fifty-five, is in therapy following a divorce. She confesses that she has always felt 'on the wrong side of a barrier, cutting her off from the real life she was meant to be living' (p.27). When asked what 'real life' entails, Jane recounts a version of the morning at Nigel's house in which she stays with Daniel and Fiona. The counsellor's professional – or perhaps salacious – interest in Jane's memory, paired with Daniel's complete lack of recollection (revealed in a kind of epilogue), offers a gently tragic view of the significance of the experience. For Jane, the memory of her 'early initiation' (p.27) into adulthood has irrevocably marked her, shaping her conservatism. However, the aesthetic nature of the image, with the sunlight and the drifting curtains, creates an ambivalence in its meaning – it is simultaneously one of exquisite beauty and pain.

Key point

It would be simplistic to read Jane as a victim in this story. She is undoubtedly naive and vulnerable, but she offers herself determinedly to Daniel as an active participant in her coming-of-age experience, keenly aware of the effects she has on him. Ambiguity remains as to the extent to which Jane is exploited, an uncertainty symbolised by the murky pool in which she swims.

Key vocabulary

Cerulean: a deep sky-blue.

Limpid: clear or transparent.

Q Why do you think this story has been chosen as the first in the collection?

Q How does the use of prolepsis (flashforward) to both Jane's and Daniel's future lives alter your understanding of the significance of Jane's sense of betrayal?

The Stain (pp.31–55)

Summary: *Marina takes a job as housekeeper for a difficult old man, an émigré from South Africa. He touches Marina inappropriately, but she rebuffs him and maintains a strictly professional relationship. He offers small gifts and promises to leave Marina the grand but dilapidated house, causing conflict with his family. She discovers that the old man was active in the South African Defence Force, and accused of an unspecified atrocity. When he passes away, Marina is bequeathed the house but refuses it.*

Taking a different approach to 'An Abduction', 'The Stain' nevertheless explores the ways in which gender, class and power interact within relationships.

Marina's relationship with the old man is contrasted with that of Wendy, his daughter, who is 'embarrassed' and 'awkward' around him (p.37). Marina, on the other hand, shares a degree of warmth and intimacy with him, albeit underpinned by the commercial nature of their relationship. She is made uncomfortable, though, when the old man emotionally comments on her 'goodness' despite her lack of social 'advantage' (p.48). Although intended to shame his own family, Marina is embarrassed by the reminder of their class difference as much as by his emotion.

As in 'An Abduction', it would be simplistic to read Marina as exploited. Although she 'needed the money' (p.31), Marina demonstrates agency, fending off the old man's wandering hands and refusing his offers of money and gifts. When accused of 'scheming' to claim the house (p.43), Marina resigns, standing up to Wendy and her son Anthony. Nevertheless, the old man's actions frequently stray into the unwanted and inappropriate and, after the party, Anthony coerces Marina into his car under the pretext of a discussion, driving off against her will. Readers are reminded of the vulnerability of women, despite their strength and resilience.

The house is a potent symbol, representing to Marina's childhood self 'all the grandeur and beauty she could imagine' (p.32). In reality, it is 'dingy and half furnished and needed a coat of paint' (pp.32–3), the polysyndeton (the insertion of conjunctions to slow the rhythm of prose) emphasising the extent to which the house fails to match Marina's fantasy. It becomes a symbol of her disillusionment with the lecherous old man and his family, with her own naivety, and also with her fantasy of bridging their social division. Wendy's subsequent restoration of the house reflects the way in which the wealthy maintain their privilege, but for Marina the house and all it represents has been corrupted, and she refuses Wendy's guilty offer of financial compensation.

Key point

The dead animal in the woods is a key symbol in this story. Marina realises that she 'couldn't undo the knowledge of the thing with the same calm ease with which [she] had taken it in' (p.52). Learning the truth of the old man's past similarly causes her to re-evaluate her relationship with him, her naivety now seeming 'wilful' (p.52).

Q How does Marina's refusal of the inheritance shape your understanding of her relationship with the old man and his family?

Q In what ways do the actions of the old man and his grandson Anthony illustrate ways in which women are sometimes treated by men?

Deeds Not Words (pp.57–65)

Summary: *Laura Mulhouse, a teacher at St Clements, is arrested as a suffragette, which inspires the schoolgirls to support the WSPU cause. Edith Carew, a colleague, engages in an affair with another teacher, Fitzsimmon Briers. When war breaks out, Fitzsimmon accepts a commission in the army, ending his relationship with Edith. Laura returns to school, traumatised from being force-fed while on a hunger strike, and Edith recognises parallels in how they have both been abused.*

Setting 'Deeds Not Words' in 1914, in the context of the early women's liberation movement, draws attention to the ways in which women have historically been disempowered within Western society. Following stories set in the 1960s and in contemporary times, the choice encourages readers to draw parallels between historical experiences and those of the present. In all three stories, tensions are established between notions of female agency, its oppression, and the consequences of the choices women make.

Women's sexuality is again a focus in this story, and Edith and Fitzsimmon's lovemaking in the French office is depicted as transformative, with Edith hardly able to believe that the 'prosaically ordinary' space could be 'the scene of such revelations' (p.60). Nevertheless, she is 'haunted by the perils of their situation' in which 'they might be found out, and she would be disgraced' (p.60). The shift in pronoun is significant: while both participants would lose their jobs, the burden of their relationship would fall more heavily on Edith. Although a willing participant in the affair, the consequences for Edith are more pronounced.

In all three stories so far, women have been pitted not only against men, but also each other. In 'An Abduction', Fiona contributes to Jane's hurt as much as Daniel; in 'The Stain', Wendy can be vicious and accuses Marina of impropriety. Here, it is the protagonist Edith who is cruelly dismissive of her colleague Laura's imprisonment, arguing she 'can't help what Miss Mulhouse chooses to do with her spare time' when invited to sign a petition calling for her release (p.62) – despite later comparing the emotional consequences of her own rejection with Laura's abuse by the authorities.

Some might consider the ending of an affair into which Edith willingly entered to be nothing like Laura's arrest and torture for a cause of which Edith 'was too sceptical to be an enthusiast' (p.58), while others may see parallels in the casual way in which the women are discarded – Edith by Fitzsimmon and Laura by both the WSPU and the students whose attention quickly shifts to the war effort. The third-person perspective suggests it is their being 'broken' and 'their shame' that unites them, with Laura unable to affect social change or maintain her hunger strike, and Edith having 'forfeited the white flower of a blameless life' (p.64). What is undeniably comparable between the two is the inequality that exists between men and women, and the ways in which women are punished for desiring the same rights and experiences as men.

Key vocabulary

Automatic writing: writing produced involuntarily, typically when channelling a spirit during a seance.

Furore: a public uproar.

Unchaste: characterised by sexual suggestiveness.

Q Do you think Edith's and Laura's experiences are similar?

Q How is the title of the story significant?

One Saturday Morning (pp. 67–86)

Summary: *Ten-year-old Carrie is practising the piano when a family friend, Dom, arrives unexpectedly. Suddenly shy, Carrie waits upstairs until her parents return and Dom reveals that his wife has died. At a dinner party that night, Carrie observes Dom embrace and kiss her mother. Her mother gently resists and, escaping upstairs, enjoys a quiet moment with her children.*

Like 'An Abduction', 'One Saturday Morning' presents a 1960s child protagonist beginning to engage with adult experience. Unlike Jane, however, Carrie remains an observer, clinging to a precarious innocence in the face of a glimpse into an adult world of intimacy.

Carrie is quiet and shy. Despite this exterior, her burgeoning sexuality is evident in letters 'full of rude words and innuendo' (p.69) that she swaps with her friend Susan. She coaxes Dom into the house, and his description draws attention to his adult masculinity, both in the smell of his sweat and a physique 'that makes a man seem fearless' (p.72). Later, Carrie is aware of 'her nakedness under her nightdress' as she examines her mother's dressing table (p.82) during the dinner party. Spying Dom kiss her mother in a desire for consolation, however, is confronting, leaving Carrie feeling 'disembodied' (p.84). She seems to pull back from her observation of Dom and her mother, wondering if she had only imagined it, as if not quite ready to venture into their adult world.

The threshold between childhood and adulthood is evident in several ways, some of which are outlined below.

- Carrie's letters are crude in their sexual humour and Carrie later recognises her 'wrong judgement' (p.84) about what is amusing and what is shaming.
- Carrie realises 'how inadequate she was to entertain [Dom]' (p.73) in stark contrast to her mother's hosting skills.
- Dom's piano playing reflects an 'adult competence, so rich in understanding' (p.75) in contrast to Carrie's childish attempts.
- Carrie feels foolish in failing to recognise or respond to Dom's grief.
- Carrie is relegated to her bedroom while the adult party takes place.
- Carrie's venturing into her mother's bedroom suggests curiosity about womanhood.

Carrie is offered a bewildering glimpse into an adult world. She 'wished fiercely that she'd never learned about Helen's death' (p.78) and, while horrified for Dom's loss, her response is shaped by something 'more selfish and self-protective' (p.78). Her later observation of Dom holding and kissing her mother, craving comfort, shocks her, and when her mother comes upstairs, Carrie realises that she too is unsettled by Dom and his 'hunger' (p.85). The happiness Carrie feels as she shares in an intimate moment with her mother and brother Paul, observing an insect that has landed on Paul's book, is sharpened by its 'precariousness' (p.86) and the realisation that there exists adult knowledge about relationships and intimacy 'unavailable to children' (p.86). The insect, extraordinary and lascivious (p.85), becomes symbolic of this adult knowledge intruding on the children's space: fascinating yet somehow grotesque.

Key point

This story highlights the relationship between mothers and daughters, and the role this plays in communicating knowledge about female sexuality. Carrie is aware of her mother's attractiveness and her ease in managing men, but also her fear of Dom. This knowledge relating to a woman's potential power over men remains mysterious to Carrie, symbolised by the 'meaning that was hidden' in the ephemera of the items on her mother's dressing table (p.82).

Q How does Carrie compare to the young protagonist of 'An Abduction'?

Q How do Carrie's crude letters contrast with her mother's more nuanced understanding of sexuality?

Key vocabulary

Austere: severe, strict or grave in appearance.

Bohemianism: unconventional behaviour, especially of an artist.

Incommensurate: disproportionate.

Lasciviously: indicating sexual interest or desire.

Experience (pp.87–111)

Summary: *After the breakdown of her marriage, Laura moves into Hana's house while Hana goes to America. Visited by Hana's ex-lover Julian, Laura seduces him. On Hana's return, Laura finds a job and moves out. Asked by Hana about Julian, Laura remains silent.*

The only story told in first person, 'Experience' represents a departure from the more observational perspective of the preceding stories. Nevertheless, it too presents readers with a naive character hungering for adult experience.

Laura is intrigued yet intimidated by Hana's confidence, her living 'flamboyantly on display' (p.88). Hana seems brash and sensual in contrast with Laura, who gets undressed in the bathroom to avoid being seen. In Hana's absence, however, her house represents a place where Laura can reinvent herself, a 'nowhere' where she is 'nobody' (p.89). Its expensive furniture, fridge stocked with exotic foods, and fashionable wardrobe seem antithetical to her own experience, which can be summed up in the 'couple of boxes of things [she'd] salvaged' from her marriage (p.89), containing pebbles, framed photographs and an empty perfume bottle of her mother's.

In a locked attic, Laura finds pornographic videos, and also diaries detailing Hana's exploits with the married Julian. 'I've never lived' (p.93), Laura thinks, comparing her conventional marriage with Hana's affair. Although thinking it 'silly' and 'demeaning' from the outside (p.94), Laura nonetheless recognises the affair as an expression of sensuous life, however 'garish' and 'exaggerated' (p.93).

Laura sees Hana's confident sexuality as a model of womanhood to which she aspires. This is evident in:

- her description of Hana's outfits as 'a performance' (p.90)
- the nature of Hana's decor, which suggests a set or stage
- the descriptions of the attic and its key as being from 'a novel or a pantomime' (p.90)
- the references to films and DVDs.

When Julian arrives unexpectedly, Laura welcomes the opportunity to try out a new persona. She borrows Hana's cosmetics and clothing, feeling like 'a little girl playing in [her] mother's clothes', albeit 'replete with new knowledge' (p.99). When she nearly faints from hunger, Julian is solicitous, insisting on making her dinner, a seduction to which Laura is 'ready to submit' (p.103). As Laura has consciously shaped her persona for Julian, having 'disguised' herself and now choosing to 'perform a part' (p.102), ambiguity arises as to whether the fainting episode is genuine or part of her performance.

Nonetheless, Laura is starving, her physical hunger metaphoric of her desire for experience. Echoing Jane, Laura too wants 'to cross the threshold and be initiated into real life' (p.106), as experienced by those who have '[given] themselves over to their erotic lives' (p.105) in contrast to her relative inexperience, which she sees as something 'maimed or unfinished' within herself (p.106). When Julian ultimately declines Laura's romantic invitation, she feels 'skinned and turned inside out' (p.109). Afterwards, she is surprised to find her thoughts settle not on 'despair' but 'hard, bleak, grey, satisfactory freedom' (p.109). Stripping off her costume, Laura finds comfort in the mementos she originally felt too ashamed to display in Hana's glamorous house. The authenticity of the experiences represented by these tokens becomes a consolation, in contrast to the superficiality of her attempts to live as Hana might.

This story ends, like 'The Stain', with its female protagonist seizing her autonomy. Julian has effected a transformation in Laura, from listless to assertive; yet it is not the unapologetic sexuality suggested by Hana's diaries that transforms Laura, but the cessation of the 'strain of yearning' for experience (p.109). Laura finds a job and her own apartment and when Hana finally asks about Julian, Laura notes that she 'wanted to be guileless, transparent' (p.111) but instead keeps the truth of the evening's events from her. Hana senses Laura's equivocation, and 'her watchfulness had respect and even fear in it' (p.111). Laura no longer feels inadequate in comparison with Hana but is now her equal, with her own secret knowledge. This ending, as with many of Hadley's stories, generates ambivalence for the reader: while Laura has gained confidence and autonomy, her rejection by Julian ironically satisfying her desire for experience, it has arguably come as a result of invading Hana's privacy and being dishonest with her.

Q In what ways does Hana function as a foil to Laura?

Q How do you compare the experiences of Laura with Jane in 'An Abduction'?

Bad Dreams (pp.113–26)

Summary: *A child wakes up in the night from a nightmare in which she dreams of an epilogue to her favourite novel,* Swallows and Amazons. *The epilogue bluntly details the inglorious deaths of most of her favourite characters: only the bland, domestic Susan lives to old age. Disturbed, the girl overturns the furniture in the living room. Later, her mother wakes and, surveying the mess, thinks it was caused by her husband.*

This eponymous story picks up on themes established in the previous stories: coming of age, secrets and their impact, and the roles to which women are expected to conform. Contextual clues suggest the story is set in the late 1950s. The furniture seems to be mid-century in design, while the wife compares herself to Monica Vitti, an actress who came to attention in that era, and wears L'Air du Temps, a perfume released in 1948. The men in the art classes she attended before marrying have returned from national service in Malaya and India, a practice that began in 1947.

The unnamed child wakes, distressed, having imagined a strange epilogue to her favourite book, *Swallows and Amazons*, an adventure story for children. She and her friends play-act the characters: 'All of them wanted to be Nancy Blackett, the strutting pirate girl' (p.115), suggesting that the young girls see as their hero a confident and non-conforming young woman. In the dreamed epilogue, however, Nancy dies after a long illness, and other characters are eradicated in a 'litany of deaths' (p.116). Tellingly, the only surviving character is Susan, 'the dullest of the Swallows', characterised as 'tame and sensible, in charge of cooking and housekeeping' (p.116). Reinforcing an internalisation of gender ideologies, the dream suggests that the only way a girl/woman can survive is by submitting to a life of domesticity. However, the thought of living to a 'ripe old age' (p.116) in such a manner fills the girl with more horror than the various deaths. The transgressive nature of resisting the normative domestic role is recognised by the girl, and she stays silent, feeling 'alone in her own home' (p.116).

The child wanders the claustrophobic basement flat, noting symbols of her parents' 'unfathomable adult preoccupations' (p.119). She is wary of the pins scattered around her mother's sewing, which is suggestive of her anxieties about submitting to a domestic role. Her father, a teacher and university student, is writing about *Leviathan*, Thomas Hobbes' treatise on social contract theory. The child feels 'a pang of fear' for her father, perhaps as a result of his somewhat untraditional masculinity: studying, playing with his daughter, his draft thesis making him 'exposed and vulnerable' (p.119). Notably, this is a fear that she does not feel for her 'capable' and gender-conforming mother (p.119). Nevertheless, this is a patriarchal household, the father's studies dictating the silence of his wife and children.

The house itself, however, is made 'uncanny' by the nightmare (p.118), and the girl feels the furniture in the living room is 'more substantial ... than she was herself' (p.120), suggesting her sense of oppression. Just as she recognises in her parents' possessions a past 'that she could never enter', the girl realises that this transgressive moment is a threshold from an innocent past to which 'she would never be able to return' (p.119). Unwilling to conform to the ordered nature of the adult world, the girl tips over the loungeroom furniture, 'her whole body [rejoicing] in the chaos' (p.120).

What was intended as a moment of rebellion, however, has deeper ramifications. Upon waking, the mother surveys the living room with horror. This disarray brings to the surface suppressed frustrations: her husband is a 'stranger' whose distance seems 'a punishment, directed at her' (p.121). She interprets the disarray as an expression of his resentment at their conventionally domestic life. She feels anger at giving up her art classes in the face of male students. Chillingly, ending this marriage does not appear a consideration. Instead, the mother sees the future 'with great clarity', one in which 'her husband was her enemy' (pp.124–5). Rather than disturbing the woman further, however, this clarity allows her to sleep blissfully.

The final paragraphs present a mundane breakfast scene. Nonetheless, this is imbued with gothic horror stemming from the secrets kept by the characters. The mother's actions of cooking breakfast for her husband and organising her children are tainted by our understanding of her rationalisation of the night's events; it is as if everyday life has now become the bad dream of the title.

Key point

This story is unusual in its sudden shift in perspective. After the little girl returns to bed, the story shifts to her similarly unnamed mother, also waking disturbed. Hadley creates a parallel between these two female characters, and their responses to the 'bad dreams' they experience. The little girl sleeps peacefully, having upended the status quo, whereas her mother claims a different kind of power in her silent defiance and resilience.

Q Why do you think the title of this story was chosen as the title of the collection?

Q How does the shift in perspective encourage you to review the child's innocent actions?

Flight (pp.127–52)

Summary: *Claire returns to London on business and decides to visit the family home, occupied by her estranged sister, Susan. Susan's children Ryan and Amy; Amy's boyfriend, Ben; and Amy and Ben's new baby live there also.*

In this story, Claire and Susan have fallen out over the ownership of the family home in Leeds. Susan moved into the home following her divorce, caring for their parents while Claire was living in London. When their parents died, Claire asked Susan to buy out her share of the home, in order to fund a deposit for a London flat. Susan sees Claire as 'monstrous in [her] selfishness' (p.143), and their relationship has not recovered.

The two women are character foils drawing attention to the outcomes of their choices, as seen in the points below.

- Claire seems affluent, with her designer handbags and expensive gifts for her family, while the depiction of Susan's home suggests the working class, with the same 'cheap wood veneer' cabinets their mother chose in the 1980s (p.136).
- Claire works professionally, an account manager for an international company, while Susan 'work[s] as a carer' (p.139), while also taking care of Ryan, Amy and Ben.
- Claire is portrayed as an exoticism, a sophisticated international jetsetter, while Susan is an exhausted and familiar 'mother figure' (p.139).
- Claire is awkward with the baby, whereas Susan – like Amy and Ben – is comfortable and nurturing.

Claire's life seems somewhat superficial and lonely, with its regrettable one-night stand and her familial relationships maintained through social media. Despite the mundane nature of Susan's family life, it seems authentic and warm. While initially one might read Claire's life as aspirational, it lacks the joy and vibrancy of Susan's, representing a complex commentary on domestic life. The scarf, a gift for Susan, is returned unopened, becoming a symbol of not only Susan's rejection of Claire, but also of her materialistic lifestyle, and a reminder of all Claire has 'lost and left behind' (p.152). Claire's ability to 'push that sorrow down and bury it' (p.152) suggests that she feels the loss of family connection deeply.

Key vocabulary

Frowsty: musty or unpleasant smelling.

Sanctimonious: making a hypocritical or public show of piety or righteousness.

Q What evidence does the story give that Susan has reluctantly submitted to the norms she initially resisted?

Q What is suggested by Claire's moment of sorrow 'for everything she'd lost and left behind' and her decision to 'push that sorrow down' (p.152)?

Under the Sign of the Moon (pp.153–82)

Summary: *Greta is on a train to visit her daughter in Liverpool when she meets Mitchell, an odd and old-fashioned young man who tries to engage her in conversation. He invites her to meet for coffee, which she initially declines. After spending some time with her daughter Kate and son-in-law Boyd, Greta goes out and encounters Mitchell, during which she is shocked when he puts his head in her lap.*

A feature of this story is the analepsis (flashback) in which the reader gains insight into Greta's first, unconventional 'marriage' to Ian in the 1970s. The unconventionality is driven by Ian, who advocates sexual freedom and takes drugs, and refers to Greta as 'bourgeois' (p.165) for her prudishness. Through his eyes, Greta sees herself as 'stiff and mechanical, inhibited' (p.166). Because of 'her background, or perhaps just because of her intrinsic nature' (p.166), she is unwilling to consummate their marriage in front of their 'wedding' guests, and he subsequently sleeps with one of those guests instead. Despite this, Greta welcomes him back to her own bed. While Ian's actions can be read as selfish, Greta is presented as an active participant, avoiding a simple characterisation as passive victim.

This relationship is contrasted with Greta's current, legal marriage to Graham, which is one of 'domestic routines' (p.167). Graham is Ian's polar opposite, but Greta still 'yearn[s], treacherously' for Ian (p.168), suggesting tension in her complex desire for both the conventional and transgressive.

What Mitchell is seeking from Greta remains ambiguous, as his social awkwardness makes it difficult to discern whether he is attracted to Greta or whether he sees her as a maternal figure. Certainly, the book he gives her, with his mother's name inscribed in it, would suggest a filial interest. Greta, however, appears to read his intention as possibly romantic, despite her dissembling thought that his attraction to her 'was out of the question' (pp.157–8) at her age. When she ventures into Liverpool to meet him, she dresses in her 'nicest outfit' and carefully applies make-up (p.175). Although she fails to meet at Mitchell's suggested location, she invites him to join her when she sees him passing by, recognising their common loneliness. She is both excited and repelled by his interest in her, perhaps motivated by the same yearning for unconventionality that spurs her desire for Ian, or perhaps as a result of facing her mortality, yet she is humiliated when he places his head in her lap in a gesture both childlike and sexual.

Key point

The manipulation of chronology in 'Under the Sign of the Moon' allows readers to observe Greta's life at contrasting points, noting the complexity of the layers of history and experience that have shaped who Greta is today.

Q How does the contrast between Greta's past and present lives shape how you interpret her interest in Mitchell?

Q In what ways can the motif of railway history be read as symbolic of the persistence of Greta's past within her present self?

Her Share of Sorrow (pp.183–94)

Summary: *Ruby and her family go on holiday, and in the attic of the house where they stay, she discovers a collection of books that she voraciously reads. Inspired, she begins writing her own novel, but when her family find her efforts amusing, she kills off her characters.*

Ruby feels like an outsider in her own family, a 'changeling' who lacks her overachieving family's artistic talents (p.183). Discovering a collection of Victorian sensation fiction, Ruby finds herself transported. The novels represent experiences unlike those in children's books, which seem to her 'too drearily like her own real-life childish routines of home and school and family' (p.188). 'Her Share of Sorrow' explores the notion of secret adult knowledge being denied to children. Like Carrie in 'One Saturday Morning', Ruby is struck by the knowledge of death, in this case of a child character in one of the novels, feeling that 'something raw and wild had been dragged from where it was concealed, into the daylight' (p.189). And like the unnamed little girl in 'Bad Dreams', this is knowledge she wishes to keep to herself, reading only in secret. When the end of the holiday disrupts her reading, Ruby feels in 'exile from her whole self' (p.190) – that is, until she begins to write her novel.

When her enthusiasm overwhelms her caution and she tells her family about her writing, they beg her to share it. Some flash of insight, however, leads Ruby to keep it private, feeling her story needs 'protection' (p.191). Her forethought proves prescient, as when her brother Nico finds her novel and reads it aloud, her family struggle to contain their mirth at her melodramatic and naive writing. Ruby is distraught, feeling 'they had hollowed out the best thing she'd ever done' (p.194). However, the story retains its hold over her, and Ruby persists in completing the novel, albeit in a far different direction. She afflicts her characters with a strange wasting fever, killing them off one by one.

In this story, the concluding line is affirmative. Ruby overcomes her shame and retains her new-found love of writing, feeling 'love, and writerly triumph' (p.194), and laying claim to her own position within her artistically oriented family. Ruby's persistence in the face of being mocked is celebrated and she emerges not cowed, but triumphant.

Key point

Clear parallels can be drawn with 'Bad Dreams', both stories featuring children and novels with tragic endings. While both stories highlight the pleasure in reading, the juxtaposition between a child and the suffering of characters draws attention to a recurring theme throughout the collection: the journey from innocence to experience. Like readers of this collection, the children find in these books representations of human suffering that recalibrate our understandings of innocence, suggesting that knowledge, however painful, is preferable to ignorance.

Key vocabulary

Aureole: a circle of radiance or light around a figure or object.

Changeling: in folklore, a child swapped with a fairy child.

Q How does this story suggest the transformative power of literature?

Silk Brocade (pp.195–215)

Summary: *Ann Gallagher, a dressmaker, is asked to make a wedding dress for Nola Higgins. Nola invites Ann and her business partner Kit, along with Kit's boyfriend Ray and a young man named Donny Ross, to a picnic at Thwaite Park, ostensibly to source more fabric for the wedding dress. Years later, Ann makes a jacket from the fabric for her daughter Sally, Nola having passed away before the dress could be made. Sally works at an event held at Thwaite Park and accidentally leaves the jacket behind.*

Like many of the characters in 'Bad Dreams', Ann has attempted to craft for herself an identity outside that which was expected of her. A dressmaker with a 'glamorous new style of … life' (p.197), she has attempted to leave her childhood in working-class Fishponds far behind her and forge a career as a fashion designer with her more outgoing friend, Kit Seaton. She feels only brief pangs of envy when asked to design wedding gowns for clients, believing that a better future lies ahead of her, talent and hard work allowing her to transcend the limitations of class and gender expectations. Nevertheless, like characters that preceded her, Ann later finds herself in a conventional marriage, raising children, her dreams of being a designer discarded.

Ann initially judges Nola based on their shared past in Fishponds. It is Kit who realises that Nola is marrying into a prestigious family, and they agree to make Nola's dress from some fabric stored in her fiancé's country manor. Ann and Kit are not selfless; they are excited at the prospect of their design being showcased at a society wedding.

An important theme in this story is the idea of disillusionment, which figures in this story in several ways.

- At Thwaite Park, the characters discover that Blaise Perney has to open the manor to the public to make ends meet, shattering their illusion of upper-class privilege.
- Blaise met Nola when she nursed him through polio, as opposed to through heroic war injuries.
- Aiming to ingratiate herself with Blaise, Ann experiences a sudden flash of insight, realising that Nola's fiancé 'didn't like them very much' as a result of their condescension to Nola (p.211).
- Nola's tragic death (and the corresponding cancellation of the wedding dress job) means that all three of the women's dreams remain unrealised.

Despite the disappointments that occur during the afternoon at Thwaite Park, the day is still joyful and full of 'exquisite' details (p.211), suggesting that the characters are poised in a moment in which their world is full of possibilities: the attraction between Ann and Donny, a blossoming career, and new and lasting friendships.

Immediately after the picnic, however, the story jumps ahead nineteen years to 1972, a startling prolepsis that recalls the opening story in the collection. We are quickly introduced to the facts of the intervening years. Ann has married Donny Ross, raising several children with him until he left her for another woman. The prolepsis functions, much as it does in 'An Abduction', to set a significant experience within the context of Ann's later, arguably more conventional, life.

The perspective shifts too, remaining in third person limited but focalised through Ann's daughter, Sally, a device also used in 'Bad Dreams'. Instead of experiencing Ann's retrospection, the reader is presented with a new character, one who is largely ignorant of the unrealised potential symbolised by the silk brocade. It is through this dispassionate perspective that we learn Nola 'died before her wedding' (p.213) having caught diphtheria from a patient.

The fabric becomes a symbol that connects the youthful and romantic potential of Ann and Donny, and Nola and Blaise, with Sally, for whom Ann makes a jacket. When Sally tries out 'her power' on a boy 'better-looking and more dangerous' than her boyfriend (pp.214–15), she accidentally leaves the jacket, and the unrealised potential it represents, behind. The brocade thus is also 'a sign that there were other youths and other pleasures, beginnings that were never completed' (Treisman 2015).

Key vocabulary:

Brocade: a rich fabric with a woven design.

Chaise longue: an elongated chair designed for reclining.

Champs-Elysées: a fashionable major street in Paris.

Foie gras: a luxury pâté-like foodstuff made from the enlarged liver of a goose.

Palladian: a grand, austere style of architecture.

Q How does Hadley's use of prolepsis and shifting perspective encourage the reader to reconsider the events that have occurred?

Q Consider the trajectory between the collection's opening and closing stories.

CHARACTERS & RELATIONSHIPS

Studying characters and relationships within a collection of short stories requires a slightly different approach from working with a full-length text. Insights can come from drawing connections across the stories, looking at parallels and contrasts between various characters, as well as within each individual story. Look for ways to group the types of characters or relationships explored. *Bad Dreams* focuses on female protagonists, but at differing ages, social contexts, or historical periods. Characters might fit multiple groups – don't forget to analyse complexities of individual characters and not only the archetype/s they represent.

In this study guide, characters have been grouped primarily according to age, and then by the significant relationship explored within each story.

Children

Key quotes

'[S]he should be more thoroughly embarked on her teenage self, like some of the girls at school …' (p.3)

'[A] vision of what consolation might be – something headlong and reckless and sweet, unavailable to children.' (p.86)

'The audacity of it took Ruby's breath away, as if something raw and wild had been dragged from where it was concealed, into the daylight.' (p.189)

'An Abduction', 'One Saturday Morning', 'Bad Dreams' and 'Her Share of Sorrow' feature child or adolescent protagonists, while 'Silk Brocade' and 'Flight' feature young adult women as significant characters. With the exception perhaps of Amy, with a child of her own ('Flight'), each is innocent or lacking the adult knowledge of the older women around them and each demonstrates a fascination with the adult world they will soon inhabit, evident in several examples:

- Jane trying on her mother's clothes ('An Abduction')
- Carrie exploring items on her mother's dressing table ('One Saturday Morning')
- the unnamed girl in 'Bad Dreams' recognising her parents 'as individuals with their own unfathomable adult preoccupations' (p.119)
- Ruby's greedy consumption of the sensation novels ('Her Share of Sorrow')
- Sally's desire to try out 'her power' (p.215) over a boy ('Silk Brocade').

These young characters are depicted as on the precipice of adulthood, occupying a liminal space in which nascent awareness of the nature of sex and adult relationships encroaches upon their childhood innocence. This suggests both a natural curiosity about growing up, and also a specific awareness that certain forms of knowledge are denied to children.

In addition to a growing awareness of their sexuality, several child characters are confronted by human mortality:

- Carrie, through the death of Dom's wife ('One Saturday morning')
- Ruby, through the death of a child in the novel *East Lynne* ('Her Share of Sorrow')
- The unnamed girl in 'Bad Dreams', through the death of the characters in her nightmare epilogue to *Swallows and Amazons*.

These confrontations engender shock, taking Ruby's breath away, making Carrie wish 'she'd never learned about Helen's death' (p.78), and impacting the unnamed girl in the title story 'against her will' (p.115). It is not just the reality of death that confronts, however, but the realisation of their own innocence that this disturbs. Their innocent world view is shattered by the realisation that they have been cocooned within childhood and are 'inadequate' in dealing with the complexities of adulthood (p.73). Some draw back from the experience, such as when Carrie, by the end of 'One Saturday Morning', retreats into her childhood naivety, questioning 'if she'd actually seen Dom dancing on the balcony with her mother' (p.86), but others attempt to assert some form of control, such as when Ruby annihilates her characters with a strange wasting disease.

Curiously, the stories often intertwine experiences of mortality and sexuality, as Carrie witnesses Dom's grief-stricken pass at her mother, and Ruby is fascinated by the lurid sexuality found in the same sensation novels that depict a child's death. Sally in 'Silk Brocade' tries out 'her power' over a boy (p.215) at Thwaite Park, using her family connection to Nola's death to foster intimacy with him. Hadley explores these two primal forces within the human condition – sexual desire and fear of mortality – and their complex relationship. Ruby's determination to complete her own novel, replete with intimate encounters and tragic deaths, illustrates the desire of these children to master understandings that remain tantalisingly out of reach.

Key point

The use of child characters grappling with adult experiences draws attention to a key theme in the text: the transition from innocence to experience, and the unsettling nature of coming of age.

Despite their youth, the child characters demonstrate great resilience, overcoming in their own way the challenges they face. Jane calmly returns home after Daniel spurns her, Carrie sleeps peacefully after upending the furniture in response to her nightmare, while Ruby completes her novel despite her family's mirthful reaction. Hadley suggests the *potential* for children to overcome formative experiences. For Jane, in particular, the day's events with Daniel and his friends leave a lifelong impression. The fact that she has, nonetheless, made a life for herself, even if not the life she might have desired, speaks to her resilience.

Adult women

Key quotes

'She couldn't forgive herself for her innocence, which seemed wilful in retrospect.' (p.52)

'I told myself that this house was a good place for me, temporarily: this nowhere where I was nobody.' (p.89)

'She felt a moment's stabbing sorrow for everything she'd lost and left behind. But she knew from past experience how to push that sorrow down and bury it.' (p.152)

Many of the adult women in these stories can also be considered innocent, or on the precipice of new understandings. In some cases, the innocence seems a choice, as it is for Laura in 'Experience', who, although aware of others' sexual proclivities, has only had sexual relations 'in the ordinary sense' (p.94); in some the innocence is 'wilful' (p.52), as it is for Marina ('The Stain'). In others it results more from ignorance or isolation. Edith in 'Deeds Not Words', for example, lives in an era where female sexuality is a taboo topic, and thus finds her love affair a series of 'revelations' (p.60) after initially fearing that her body 'would bloom and fade under her clothes without any man ever knowing it' (p.59).

The characters who seem most unhappy are those who have submitted to the social norms of their British context, particularly regarding marriage and motherhood, following glimpses into a more unconventional world. Jane's therapy session reveals her dissatisfaction with her conventional life, her fantasy of quietly joining Daniel and Fiona in the bedroom suggesting a long-repressed desire to have entered the casually transgressive world they represent, to have made different choices in that formative moment. The mother in 'Bad Dreams' recalls with regret the art classes that she gave up, and although Greta ('Under the Sign of the Moon') seems generally happy with Graham, she cannot put aside her attraction to the unconventional Ian and allows herself to be caught up in her curiosity for Mitchell.

Although some characters are disappointed by the knowledge they gain, several draw strength from experience and emerge renewed in their own sense of self:

- Marina, furious at realising her naivety, stands firm in her resolve to refuse the inheritance out of a sense of pride and self-respect ('The Stain')
- Laura overcomes her ennui and finds new purpose following Julian's rejection ('Experience')
- The unnamed wife in 'Bad Dreams' is exhilarated at her clear, albeit misguided, insight into her strained marriage.

The women in these stories suggest a desire for experience or intimacy. Often, though, they seem shamed for their attempts to fulfil such desires. In 'Deeds Not Words', Edith is shamed by her participation in the affair with Fitzsimmon, and the understanding that as a result of the affair, 'he had power over her' (p.64). Similarly, Greta in 'Under the Sign of the Moon' is left 'burning with humiliation' after Mitchell shocks her by placing his face in her lap (p.181), and even the seemingly brazen Hana hides the evidence of her sexual life away in the attic and censors the erotic language in her diaries. Children, too, are shamed: Ruby is laughed at for her novel, while Jane is rejected by Daniel in favour of Fiona.

Mother–daughter relationships

Key quotes

'Her mother's mild voice was in her ear, incurious: they had begun to wonder where she was.' (p.21)

'Carrie fingered the objects on her mother's dressing table, so well known they seemed like parts of her own self ...' (p.82)

'Scrupulously, because they read all the right guides to parenting, Adrian and Dalia ignored Ruby's greedy eating at the supper table.' (p.184)

Mother–daughter relationships are depicted in several stories. In 'An 'Abduction' and 'Her Share of Sorrow', children feel unsupported by their mothers. Jane initially admires her mother, noting that she 'looked just like her' (p.2); in contrast Ruby 'looked like a changeling' (p.183) and her mother's physical opposite. Both, however, are let down by their mothers; Jane's fails to register alarm at her daughter's disappearance and Ruby's mother is awkward around her daughter, learning parenting from manuals and unable to control her mirth at the girl's naive writing.

In contrast, the unnamed girl in 'Bad Dreams' sees her mother as 'the whole world' (p.119), and in 'One Saturday Morning', Carrie seems equally attached to her mother, particularly evident in their closeness within the final image of the story. 'Silk Brocade' also depicts a warm mother–daughter relationship, with Sally and Ann 'absorbed together ... in projects of transformation' following the breakdown of Ann's marriage (p.212). What is common across the collection is the significance their mothers hold for these impressionable young girls; through their attention or emotional distance mothers shape their children's identities.

'Flight' and 'Under the Sign of the Moon' reveal that relationships between mothers and adult daughters are also imperfect, with Susan 'disappointed' over Amy not going to college (p.134) and unhappy with her daughter's choice of partner, whom she blames for Amy's 'lack of ambition' (p.137). Similarly, Greta and Kate's relationship does not seem close; they 'weren't ... the kind of mother and daughter who were always cuddling and touching' (p.158) and Greta recognises her daughter's faults within her marriage. Despite this, the relationships are far from strained; Susan welcomes not only Amy into the family home, but also Amy's boyfriend and new baby. Similarly, recovering from cancer treatment, Greta travels to Liverpool to stay with her daughter, suggesting that the bonds between mothers and daughters remain strong.

Intimate relationships

Key quotes

'It had never occurred to her until now that the masculine ... could be so intimately important, in relation to herself ...' (p.11)

'[I]n her dream she had seemed to fit against the shape of him as sweetly as a nut into its shell, losing herself inside him. But now he was lost, somewhere she couldn't follow him.' (p.121)

Many of the stories in this collection reveal the ways in which female identity can be formed in relation to the men in their lives. Often this relationship has undertones of coercive patriarchal control or even explicit manipulation. Although a willing participant, Jane ('An Abduction') is used by the older Daniel who takes advantage of her desire for experience, before discarding her in favour of Fiona. Marina, in 'The Stain', finds herself subject to the old man's inappropriate touching, although she is confident enough to reproach him. Initially she dismisses it as a simple desire for physical contact, but later she revises her impression, recognising the old man's 'leering, repulsive side' and regretful of her permissive indulgence of his actions (p.52). Other examples include:

- Edith's recognition that Fitzsimmon holds all the power in their relationship ('Deeds Not Words')
- Ian's criticism of Greta's values as bourgeois ('Under the Sign of the Moon')
- Ann's desire to transform herself after her marriage breakdown ('Silk Brocade').

Many of the women experience broken marriages: we learn, for example, that Jane's marriage breaks down later in life ('An Abduction'), as does Ann's in 'Silk Brocade'. Laura in 'Experience' comes to stay with Hana after her own marriage breakdown. Those who stay together are often troubled: Greta ('Under the Sign of the Moon') yearns for her transgressive relationship with Ian, despite her pleasant marriage to

Graham. Although the marriage does not break up in 'Bad Dreams', it is reduced to one of 'silent violence', as suppressed grievances rise to the surface (p.125). In many of these relationships, it is submitting to convention that troubles the women. Jane feels she has been cut off from the 'real life she was meant to be living' (p.27). The mother in 'Bad Dreams' feels rage at her husband for what she imagines is his criticism of his own domestication, 'as if she didn't feel fed up sometimes' (p.124), and Greta and Graham's marriage is one of 'domestic routines' (p.167).

Key point

The collection does reflect genuine warmth within some marriages. Marina's sympathy for the old man's loneliness prompts her appreciation that her own body felt 'luxuriantly wrapped in touching' (p.40), by her husband and her child. Similarly, both Ruby's and Carrie's parents' relationships seem positive.

Women and other women

Key quotes

'Marina didn't take offence when Wendy tried ordering her around, finding fault.' (p.36)

'[T]hey would surely be able to find their way through all this rubble of the past piled up between them.' (p.149)

A number of stories feature relationships between female characters who are not family. While these relationships may be amicable, there is often an undercurrent of tension arising from some sort of competition or comparison between them. In 'An Abduction', Jane and the more worldly Fiona compete for Daniel's attention. Initially, Jane accepts the 'justice' of her 'defeat' at the hands of the 'older, prettier, more sophisticated girl' (p.17), although, attracted by her guilelessness in contrast to Fiona's deliberate 'manoeuvring' (p.19), Daniel chooses to sleep with Jane. The next morning, when Jane discovers Daniel and Fiona asleep together, she again accepts her defeat, quietly withdrawing and returning home. In 'Experience', there is a similar competition as Laura attempts to seduce Hana's ex-lover. Despite Julian ultimately declining Laura's advances, Laura's choice to wear Hana's clothing suggests an attempt to mimic the other woman and her experiences.

Although not competing for romantic attention, in 'The Stain', Marina and Wendy find themselves in conflict over their relationship with Wendy's father. Marina develops a warmer relationship with the old man than his own daughter; despite biological connection, he and Wendy are described as 'almost strangers' (p.37). Recognising his depression, Marina cares for the old man, encouraging him to interact with her own son, taking him to church, and preparing his preferred food. When the old man wants to leave Marina his house, Wendy is first furious, then contrite, knowing that she is unlikely to find another carer for her difficult father.

In 'Deeds Not Words', Edith disapproves of both her colleague Laura's suffragette politics and her friendliness with students. When her heart is broken by the ending of her illicit affair, however, Edith draws parallels between her own shame and Laura's, the latter's spirit broken by her arrest and force-feeding, and the hiatus of the WSPU activity due to the outbreak of war.

What is notable in these stories is the absence of deep friendships between women, despite the commonality of circumstance and experience. The exception is Ann and Kit in 'Silk Brocade', but the emotional depth of the friendship is largely unexplored. Kit is godmother to Ann's daughter Sally, but the narrative frequently reveals Ann's private criticisms of Kit's infidelity and snobbery. Mostly, the women in these stories struggle through their conflicts alone, suggesting that, far from bringing individuals together through shared circumstance, the experience of womanhood can be isolating.

Key point

As Jane surmises in 'An Abduction', 'her experience was not like anyone else's' (p.25), yet clearly the stories in this collection draw attention to significant commonalities between women's experiences.

Minor male characters

Although Hadley's stories focus on the experiences of women, there are several significant male characters worth considering. It would be simplistic to read men as the 'enemy' in this collection; male characters, despite being secondary, are often equally complex and nuanced in their construction.

Some men are represented as exploitative and patriarchal, such as Daniel in 'An Abduction', Fitzsimmon in 'Deeds Not Words' and Greta's first husband Ian in 'Under the Sign of the Moon'. Although perhaps taking advantage of their respective lovers' naivety, Daniel and Fitzsimmon are not coercive or abusive, though the same cannot be said for Ian. Despite his positive characterisation, Dom's grief-driven pass at Carrie's mother in 'One Saturday Morning' is enough to create an undercurrent of fear that Carrie deduces from her mother's behaviour. The old man in 'The Stain' is similarly complex. His behaviour amounts to sexual harassment, and his offer of financial gifts to Marina problematic, yet upon his death he leaves his house to her rather than his own family, even though Marina has rebuffed his advances.

Mitchell in 'Under the Sign of the Moon' is a curious character, socially awkward and desperate to engage with Greta. His interest in the older woman is unclear, and the story never clearly resolves if his attraction is filial (i.e. seeing her as a maternal figure) or sexual. As it stands, it seems an Oedipal hybrid of the two. His characterisation, as with the old man in 'The Stain', seems to be more pathetic than threatening.

In contrast, the collection offers a number of positive male figures, such as Adrian in 'Her Share of Sorrow' and Marina's husband Gary in 'The Stain', who seems supportive and kind. The father in 'Bad Dreams' appears wrapped up in his studies but is also depicted as playful with his daughter and her friends, and while Ben in 'Flight' smokes marijuana and seems unmotivated to work hard, he is a tender and caring father.

THEMES, IDEAS & VALUES

The transition from innocence to experience

Key quotes

'[G]rown-up insight seemed to come not through gradual accretion but all at once.' (p.13)

'[A] vision of what consolation might be – something headlong and reckless and sweet, unavailable to children.' (p.86)

'I've never lived, I thought, as I knelt there ... I've never lived: the words ran in my head.' (p.93)

'[A]fter my evening with Julian I knew I came across as older and more experienced. People seemed to take me more seriously – as if I'd been initiated into something after all ...' (p.110)

Many of the characters experience a coming of age, or a transition from a state of innocence to experience. Child characters are exposed to new knowledge that reinforces the fragility of their innocence, and their growing awareness of the roles expected of them as they mature into women. Even though such adult knowledge can be unexpected or unwanted, these girls demonstrate a degree of curiosity about the nature of adulthood.

In some of the stories, children actively seek out their transition into adult sexuality. This is most evident in 'An Abduction', in Jane's acceptance of a ride with the boys. She feels trapped in a liminal state, frustrated that she has not 'more thoroughly embarked on her teenage self' (p.3). She watches the car and its driver, Daniel, 'hungrily' (p.9), and later engages in 'clumsy arrangements' (p.24) with him that leave her 'sick with desire' (p.24). While Jane's sudden 'grown-up insight' (p.13) might suggest her agency, sexual intimacy is still a 'cave of things unknown' (p.15). Her characterisation as 'afraid' (p.20), along with the story's title, generates ambiguity around the degree to which Jane is a consenting participant rather than a vulnerable girl exploited by an older male. Either way, her new acuity allows her to recognise the 'motives and relations' (p.13) of the other characters, the hierarchy between the male characters, and the subtle competition between her and Fiona.

Sally in 'Silk Brocade' similarly seeks sexual experience, seducing a boy with whom she works. As well as personal pleasure, these young women realise that their sexuality affords them a kind of power over men (although in Jane's case this power is insecure, her desire for Daniel ultimately unreciprocated). Sally's desire ends in a state of 'complications and adjustments' (p.215), suggesting that a young woman's coming of age is not without tension or conflict, and these formative experiences can have lasting implications, as the prolepsis in 'An Abduction' reveals to be true for Jane.

Other child characters retain their innocence, albeit while recognising a future into which they must one day enter. Carrie's burgeoning sexuality is apparent in her awareness of her own body and Dom's masculine presence ('One Saturday Morning'). She also recognises her mother's competent management of unwanted male attention, and is consequently ashamed of the childish and crude letters she has written. However, by the story's end, Carrie retreats to the fragile security of her childhood innocence, finding reassurance in her mother's presence. She questions whether she even saw her mother dancing with Dom, implying that adult sexuality remains a mystery 'unavailable to children' (p.86). Similarly, Ruby ('Her Share of Sorrow') grasps the sexuality of the characters in *East Lynne* only through 'a thick fog' (p.188). Their crime of adultery is 'fairly incomprehensible' (p.188), and she wonders 'what had they done wrong exactly?' (p.188). In spite of this limited awareness, Ruby attempts to replicate adult sexuality within her own novel. Ruby's mother is unwilling to broach the subject with her daughter, reflecting a cultural reluctance to discuss sexual matters with children, despite their curiosity and perhaps need for appropriate education. These stories reveal the tension between the relative freedom afforded by childhood obliviousness and an emerging sense of the potential power available in the adult world.

The value of experience

Both child and adult characters in these stories seek experience. Sometimes the nature of this experience is clearly defined, but in other cases it is a yearning for something indeterminate, something half-grasped or that might simply challenge the familiarity of the known world.

- Jane is frustrated by her transitional state as an adolescent and welcomes the experiences offered by her encounter with Daniel and his friends ('An Abduction').
- Carrie is eager to invite Dom into the house, only belatedly realising her inadequacy as a host, particularly in comparison to her accomplished mother ('One Saturday Morning').
- The little girl in 'Bad Dreams' is enthralled by the characters in *Swallows and Amazons* who cross 'the threshold of safety into a thrilling unknown' (p.115, 'Bad Dreams').
- Laura hungers for the kind of experience represented by Hana and her confident sexuality ('Experience').

Gaining experience can be revelatory, but it can also be fraught with danger. What is notable is that many characters are punished in some way for their desire for experience, often through what KJ Orr describes as being 'shamed for overreaching' (2017). Stepping outside the boundaries of what conservative society deems appropriate can result in disciplinary effects that shape the characters' sense of self. Examples of this are listed below.

- Jane is clearly distressed by Daniel's casual rejection, an experience that subsequently shapes her fears for her own daughters ('An Abduction').
- Edith finds sex with Fitzsimmon revelatory, but knows she risks both her job and social standing in pursuing the affair ('Deeds Not Words').
- Carrie is shamed by her childish failure to entertain Dom in her parents' absence or to match his talent for the piano ('One Saturday Morning').

- Greta is embarrassed at Mitchell's sudden inappropriate display when, flattered by his attention, she seeks out his company ('Under the Sign of the Moon').
- Ruby is shamed by her family for her naive writing ('Her Share of Sorrow').

What becomes clear across the collection, however, is that despite the disappointments that experience can bring, it is valued as preferable to ignorance and naivety. 'So now you know', Jane is told in 'An Abduction' (p.25), a line that could apply to most of the protagonists. For better or worse, characters come to terms with the knowledge gained from their experience, even when the consequences are detrimental or invisible to others.

Key point

Hadley reveals the renegotiation of one's understandings of oneself and one's position in the world that arises from the internalising of formative experiences. Jane, for example, reflects on 'the mystery of her changed life' (p.24), while Laura ('Experience') feels as if she has been 'initiated' into a world from which she was previously excluded (p.110).

Secrets and their revelation

Key quotes

'[Jane's] early initiation stayed in a sealed compartment in her thoughts and seemed to have no effects, no consequences.' (p.27)

'She kept her eyes on me, and her watchfulness had respect and even fear in it, as if I were the one with secrets.' (p.111)

'At any rate, nothing – nothing – would ever make her tell them that she'd done it. They would never know, and that was funny, too.' (p.120)

Secrets are a key element of the stories' gothic style, and typically revolve around personal experiences that might be considered transgressive or controversial. These secrets can sometimes weigh heavily on the characters, performing a disciplinary function by which characters conform to conventional ways of behaving. For others, the withholding of knowledge can yield a form of power or can preserve the privacy to explore one's identity without the glare of scrutiny.

'An Abduction' reveals how secrets can become a burden, shaping the identity of those who carry them. Keeping her time with Daniel a secret, Jane's eventual revelation to her therapist highlights how she has carried this moment throughout her life 'in a sealed compartment' (p.27). It 'seemed to have no effects' (p.27), but the word 'seemed' implies that there have, in fact, been significant consequences, although Jane never 'connect[ed] her fears to anything that had happened to her' (p.27). The lack of closure to Jane's therapy suggests that for her the secret remains unresolved. The ambiguity of the counsellor's comment that Jane's hesitant opening-up was 'something' (p.28) could reveal the potential for Jane's personal growth. What is clear, however, is the way in which Jane's adult life has formed around the secret she has kept.

Laura, on the other hand, finds secrets empowering ('Experience'). She basks in the 'respect' and 'fear' in Hana's gaze after keeping the truth of her encounter with Julian from her (p.111). Although 'nothing had happened' with Julian (p.110), the experience has changed not only her self-perception but also the way others now take her 'more seriously' (p.110). The use of first person in this story draws the reader clearly into Laura's state of mind and highlights her new-found confidence. Ruby ('Her Share of Sorrow') also finds solace and strength in her secrets. Laboriously working through a collection of sensation novels, Ruby finds reading transportive and inspirational, but, literally locking herself away in the attic, the experience is a private one. Disclosure risks her discoveries being 'appropriated' by others (p.190), robbing Ruby of this singular joy in her banal existence. She is moved to write her own novel and claim her place within her artistically talented family – an experience she also keeps to herself, revelling in the 'power and importance' she feels (p.191). On some level, however, she recognises her naivety, noting there was 'something delicate in her story [that] needed her protection' (p.191). The secret nature of her literary adventures provides a space to explore adult themes of sex and death without fear or shame.

The dualistic nature of secrets is most evident in 'Bad Dreams', in which the secret kept by the unnamed girl thrills and empowers her while having tragic consequences for her parents' marriage. The sudden shift in perspective midway through the story draws attention to the paradoxical nature of secrets. Frightened by her nightmare, and particularly the horror of living to 'a ripe old age' like the 'tame and sensible' Susan (p.116), when she yearns to be the pirate girl Nancy, the girl tips over the loungeroom furniture, a private moment of rebellion against the oppressive domesticity of her parents' world, restoring a sense of control rocked by the implications of her nightmare. This act leaves her giddy, and she decides to keep it from her parents, finding humour in their likely confusion. She also vows to keep her nightmare a secret, believing that saying the words aloud would somehow render them more real, or that her fears would be dismissed by her parents.

Misreading the meaning of the upturned furniture, her mother is initially unsettled by its implications. Believing it to be an act of criticism on the part of her husband, she decides to refuse to acknowledge aloud 'the message he'd left for her' (p.125), keeping to herself the 'awful truth' that 'her husband was her enemy' (p.125), a secret that she had kept even from herself, and is only now acknowledging. Instead of challenging her husband, which likely would have led to clarity that the situation was an act of childish mischief, her silence reduces their marriage to 'a long tunnel of antagonism' (p.124). The parallelism between daughter and mother, as well as the echoing line that 'nothing – nothing – would ever make [them] tell' (p.120), draws readers' attention to the ironic juxtaposition of their secrets. While the keeping of secrets can afford a kind of power or control, this can come at a devastating cost to others.

Secrets revealed

The uncovering of secrets is another example of revelatory experience that permeates the collection. When secrets are revealed, their impacts can be shocking as well as enlightening. In 'The Stain', Marina re-evaluates her relationship with the old man after his grandson, Anthony, reveals to her that rather than being a mere farmer in South Africa, he was a member of the South African Defence Force. While the details are 'pretty murky' (p.51), it is clear the old man committed some atrocity, although he received an amnesty due to his age. Anthony exposes this secret as a strategy to manipulate Marina into refusing the old man's financial gifts by appealing to her sense of morality. Like other characters, Marina is left feeling 'burdened' by the knowledge of a secret (p.51), and she is reminded of the time she unexpectedly encountered the decaying corpse of an animal on a woodland walk. In that instance, she realised that 'you couldn't undo the knowledge of the thing' (p.52) – an idea symbolically echoed when the old man dies, and the only resolution available to Marina is to refuse the house he bequeathed her.

Female sexuality

Key quotes

'Then her mother, with her hand flat on Dom's chest, was pushing him away in the teasing, charming way she pushed away the other men.' (p.84)

'But this stuff was ordinary, wasn't it? Everybody did it. What was the matter with me that I didn't take it for granted, that my heart beat stickily, as if the little sex kit had somehow made a fool of me?' (p.92)

'He hurts me and frightens me, but it's the best s*x ever.' (p.93)

There is a tension between the conventional and the sexually transgressive that runs throughout the collection. Many of the stories explore characters' intimate experiences, including first encounters, affairs with married men, a partner's infidelity and the routines of married life. As a whole, the collection argues that female sexuality is diverse and complex, and a significant factor in shaping these characters' sense of self. Examples are numerous, some of which are explored below.

- Despite her 'clumsy' loss of virginity and the ambiguity regarding her agency in 'An Abduction', Jane feels almost 'sick with desire' to repeat the transformative experience that led to a 'new self' (p.20), although she is ultimately heartbroken when Daniel returns to Fiona's bed.
- Edith's first experience with Fitzsimmon is transformative and revelatory, yet she is 'haunted by the perils of their situation' (p.60), given its illicit nature ('Deeds Not Words').
- 'The Stain' highlights the way in which women are subject to sexual harassment, as the old man frequently kisses and touches Marina, and when Anthony picks her up in his car, Marina feels threatened ('The Stain').
- Claire regrets her one-night stand with a colleague, whom 'she didn't know very well, didn't even like all that much' (p.127); the experience lingers, 'not in a pleasant way but as a bruised, raw fatigue' (p.128, 'Flight').
- The juxtaposition of Greta's relationships with men in 'Under the Sign of the Moon' illustrates the complexity of desire: Greta 'still yearned, treacherously' (p.168) for her first husband, despite his emotional cruelty, while her second marriage is represented as conventional – her meeting with Mitchell may be an attempt to feel desirable again following her illness ('Under the Sign of the Moon').
- Women realise that sex can provide a degree of influence over men, as evident in Sally 'trying her power out on this boy' (p.215); yet this power is insecure, as evident in the way that Daniel ('An Abduction') and Julian ('Experience') ultimately decline the female characters.

Desire is a powerful emotion, but one that has been policed throughout the time periods represented in the collection. Some characters have internalised a degree of shame over their sexual desires, in examples such as Laura's embarrassment at discovering Hana's diaries and toys

('Experience'), Edith's fear of discovery in 'Deeds Not Words', Greta's embarrassment over Mitchell's public intimacy ('Under the Sign of the Moon') and Jane's repression of her 'early initiation' into sex (p.27, 'An Abduction'). Additionally, in some stories, issues of sex and intimacy are closely interwoven with a critical awareness of the female body, such as the shame that Jane feels about her feet when Daniel plays with them ('An Abduction'), the 'fear or disgust' (p.155) that strikes Greta as a result of the frailty arising from treatment for a gynaecological condition ('Under the Sign of the Moon'), or the way in which the unnamed wife feels rejected by her husband's physical distance in 'Bad Dreams'. The stories in *Bad Dreams* seem to draw attention to the tensions and anxieties arising when women seek to claim their own sexuality, particularly in the face of social conventions that have historically operated to control or repress their experiences.

Domestic life

Key quotes

'[W]as the disorder a derisory message meant for her, because he despised her homemaking, her domestication of the free life he'd once had?' (p.124)

'Claire got the impression that the young parents were passing their days quite happily in this cocoon of animal warmth and smells: as if they were playing house, everything changed and simplified, revolving around the new life.' (p.134)

As befitting the collection's neodomestic genre, the majority of the stories take place in domestic settings and feature conflicts arising from domestic situations. Relationships, housework and parenting duties all feature significantly throughout. Many are depicted in rich detail, with specific descriptions of interiors or the suburban landscape. Within these depictions, however, are unsettling details: the claustrophobia of the basement flat in 'Bad Dreams'; the dingy interior of the grand house in 'The Stain' and the secret of its elderly occupant; the rabbit droppings in 'An Abduction'; the parents' guilty decision to accept Ruby's secretive behaviour in the attic because of the peace it affords them ('Her Share of Sorrow'). In a gothic sense, these details point to the corruption of the domestic idyll: manifestations of the secrets harboured beneath the facade of pleasant suburbia.

Not all stories represent domestic life as oppressive, however. Carrie's mother in 'One Saturday Morning' delights in entertaining within her home and is close with her children. Marina is similarly fulfilled by her family, and while chaotic and worn when observed through Claire's eyes, Susan's family home is full of warmth and life.

Key point

The juxtaposition of positive and oppressive domestic experiences points to an overriding theme throughout the collection, best summed up by Hadley herself in a 2016 essay for *The New Yorker*: 'This is one of the miracles that fiction works: You can be a doubter and a believer in the same moment, in the same sentence.'

Class issues

The United Kingdom is one of many societies affected by wealth inequalities and social prejudices arising from class difference. The clearest example of this is the working-class Marina ('The Stain'), who works for the wealthy old man and his daughter, Wendy. She admired the big house as a child, believing it stood for 'grandeur and beauty' (p.32) and even now, as an adult, 'she liked to stand dreaming, looking down from the windows on her old life' (p.37). When the old man decides to leave Marina the house in his will, however, she realises that she will always be presumed to be 'after his money' (p.43). Her pride and sense of morality lead her to refuse to 'touch a penny' (p.55), despite its transformative potential in her family's life.

'Silk Brocade' also highlights issues of class disparity, with Ann initially hesitant to make Nola's wedding dress because of their common history in the working-class Bristol suburb of Fishponds. Not only is Ann driven by a motivation to 'leave Fishponds behind' (p.196), she believes accepting such clientele would stymie her plans for an upwardly mobile fashion business. When Claire returns to her family home in 'Flight', bearing expensive gifts that she regards as 'currency between women' (p.128), she reflects on the working-class setting she has left behind, lingering on details such as the 'cheap wood veneer' (p.136), her observation sharpened by distance. Susan's return of the expensive silk scarf Claire bought her is as much a repudiation of Claire's class mobility as it is of her attempts at buying reconciliation, given that money lies at the heart of their estrangement. 'An Abduction' also draws attention to class distinctions, as the wealthy Patrick asks Jane if she thinks they are 'layabouts and social parasites' (p.15), after Jane comments that 'it was only fair for everyone to do a day's hard work' (p.14).

Key point

The majority of Hadley's protagonists are firmly middle class, and criticisms seem to be directed at the wealthy who are generally characterised as spoiled, superficial or even exploitative.

Other themes

As well as these significant themes, you might consider the following.

- Parenting: the tension between monitoring ones' children or allowing them the freedom to learn from their own experiences, particularly evident in 'Her Share of Sorrow' and 'An Abduction'.
- Literature: books and our literary heritage are significant to several stories, which explore the power of literature to transport readers and act as a repository of truths about human nature. 'Her Share of Sorrow' and 'Bad Dreams' clearly engage with this theme.
- History: histories and their sometimes unnoticed impacts on the present are important in several stories, whether that be personal histories ('An Abduction', 'Flight', 'Under the Sign of the Moon') or cultural histories (racial tensions in 'The Stain' or the layers of cultural history in Liverpool in 'Under the Sign of the Moon').

DIFFERENT INTERPRETATIONS

Different interpretations arise from different responses to a text. Over time, a text will evoke a wide range of responses from its readers, who may come from various social or cultural groups and live in very different places and historical periods. Responses by critics and reviewers can be published in newspapers, journals and books, both online and in print. They can also be expressed in discussions among readers in the media, classrooms, book groups and so on.

While there is no single correct reading or interpretation of a text, it is important to understand that an interpretation is more than a personal opinion – it is the justification of a point of view on the text. To present an interpretation of a text based on your point of view, you must use a logical argument and support it with relevant evidence from the text.

Critical viewpoints

Reading critical responses to your text can help your study of the text by identifying ideas, themes and textual features that you might want to analyse more deeply in your own discussions of the work, as well as by providing examples of how to support responses to a text. You might find responses that identify themes you had not considered, and you might even find responses with which you disagree; this can be an excellent way to stimulate your own thinking and analysis. If you disagree with a review, try to come up with a supported argument against it, providing examples from the text to substantiate your point of view.

Try to find a range of responses to your text, including at least some of the following:

- professional responses (i.e. those published in commercial or academic sources)

→

- personal responses (such as those on literary networking sites, or on regular literary blogs)
- reviews from Australia as well as other countries
- reviews from different perspectives (such as social/cultural).

However, remember that responses that 'like' or 'dislike' a text, without presenting a strong argument as to why, are not likely to be useful. This goes for your own analysis too: the point of studying and discussing texts is not to write about whether or not you enjoyed it, but to form responses to the work and to understand how to provide textual evidence to support these responses. Note that many critical responses are likely to contain both positive and negative feedback about a text.

The critical responses to *Bad Dreams* below provide examples of how to use textual evidence to support a perspective.

KJ Orr in *The Guardian* (a review focusing on Hadley's social commentary)

Orr praises the collection's 'nuance and psychological acuity' in representing the experience of women and girls. In a thematic reading, Orr notes that the stories principally explore the crossing of thresholds and the gaining of experience. The resulting knowledge can be 'unexpected or unwanted, and it can feel transgressive', and women can be shamed for their 'overreaching'. Orr comments on the insights gained through Hadley's sudden shifts in perspective within various stories, and how this creates tension between lived experience and external observation, from positions of 'exile, dislocation or dispossession'. Orr describes Hadley's writing as 'remarkable' in its range, encompassing 'acerbic social observation and wry humour with moments of breathtaking delicacy and tenderness'.

Claire Jarvis in the *LA Review of Books* (a review focusing on reader response)

Jarvis reads Hadley's stories through a darker lens, suggesting the collection constitutes a 'vicious catalog of the misery of women who care – for themselves, for other people, or for abstract principles like love or justice'. The stories represent often unwelcome knowledge as a stain that cannot be removed once discovered. Hadley's 'blend of familiarity and idiosyncrasy' is noted in the way mundane settings or events are rendered unsettling through 'her unwavering eye for a telling detail'. Jarvis notes the particularly British nature of the collection, in terms of settings and historical events, but especially in its literary references. There is an ambiguity in such references, as the stories suggest the characters are 'products of literary and historical pressures' while undermining the 'middlebrow condescension' aimed at those with only passing awareness of British literary history. Finally, Jarvis explores how several stories reveal 'the attenuated pleasure in cruelty that reading permits', as with Ruby in 'Her Share of Sorrow', and concludes by suggesting Hadley's ironic intention to illustrate how her own readers are fascinated by her representations of female suffering.

Sara Cutaia in the *Chicago Review of Books* (a review focusing on the craft of Hadley's stories)

Cutaia also appreciates Hadley's eye for detail and how the collection 'pulls magic from the mundane'. She argues that it is the 'clarity and confidence' in Hadley's style that allows seemingly ordinary details to engage the reader and take on extraordinary significance. Cutaia, however, feels that the narrative pace is 'sometimes a little too leisurely', making some stories less impactful or memorable than others, for example when the reveal comes too late, or the set-up is perhaps too self-indulgent. Furthermore, Cutaia finds the endings of the stories 'sometimes too abrupt, sometimes trying too hard for ambiguity', although she acknowledges that could be a strategy to emphasise 'the banality and mystery of modern life'. Overall, though, Hadley is 'a great writer', the stories have 'beauty and insight', even if not all are 'executed to fruition'.

Sarah Crown in the *Times Literary Supplement* (a review focusing on the theme of gender)

Crown is one of the many reviewers who compare Hadley's work to Alice Munro's in their focus on women and their lives. She notes how Hadley's attention to the domestic has perhaps been a barrier to greater success, but that her writing is 'finally gaining the recognition it deserves'. She notes Hadley's finely tuned sense of detail, and how certain objects recur across the collection, suggesting 'the lives of these girls and women are interlinked'. Crown describes Hadley's stories as 'investigative, rather than generative', quietly observing women's experiences and in doing so encouraging readers to confront the banality of their own lives. Crown focuses on how the collection lays bare 'the world's vast indifference' but suggests the responses of the characters are 'elevatory', bringing significance to the mundane.

Two interpretations

The following interpretations demonstrate how similar observations can be used to sustain contrasting interpretations of the text, providing they are supported with evidence from that text.

Interpretation 1: *Bad Dreams* suggests that women's experience is a catalogue of tribulations.

In this collection, the majority of stories reveal the pain, suffering or mundanity inherent in women's lives. Some characters experience painful events such as the rejection of a lover (Jane in 'An Abduction', Edith in 'Deeds Not Words' or Laura in 'Experience'), the breakdown of family relationships (Claire and Susan in 'Flight') or even physical illness (Greta in 'Under the Sign of the Moon'). Others experience significant trauma, such as Laura's force-feeding in 'Deeds Not Words' or Carrie's confrontation with mortality in 'One Saturday Morning'.

Some characters are shamed for stepping outside the boundaries of what is conventionally expected of women and girls, often for seeking sexual experience ('An Abduction', 'Deeds Not Words'), or reaching for knowledge deemed too adult for them ('Her Share of Sorrow', 'One Saturday Morning'). Sometimes this shame comes from external sources, such as parents, but sometimes it manifests as internalised patriarchal attitudes.

Women such as Ann ('Silk Brocade') and the unnamed mother in 'Bad Dreams' find themselves giving up their dreams for a different life and conforming to the stereotypical role of wife and mother. The unnamed mother, for example, feels a flash of resentment at having given up her art degree. In most of the stories, these characters are represented as victims of knowledge, their experiences resulting in a psychological burden that has shaped their identities and, in many cases, the life choices they have subsequently made.

Importantly, such suffering typically goes unnoticed by others. The sudden shift in perspective to focus on Daniel at the end of 'An Abduction' reveals how he has had 'too much happiness in his life' (p.29) to even remember Jane. For him, the girl's 'extraordinary offer of herself without reserve' is 'all just gone' (p.29). Although Edith ('Deeds Not Words') recognises Laura's suffering, her own escapes attention, as the illicit nature of her affair with Fitzsimmon means she is unable to acknowledge how 'broken' (p.65) she feels. The unnamed mother in 'Bad Dreams' is prepared to carry on at breakfast as normal, waiting for her husband to acknowledge 'the silent violence between them' (p.125), which, of course, the reader knows he never will, being innocent of the incident that has crystallised the woman's internal conflict. Her daughter, similarly, is unable to discuss her pain, feeling 'it was better to keep [it] hidden' (p.116). Jane ('An Abduction'), Ruby ('Her Share of Sorrow'), Greta ('Under the Sign of the Moon') and Claire and Susan ('Flight') also suffer in isolation, unable to talk with those who have hurt them. Instead, as Claire notes, they learn to 'push that sorrow down and bury it' (p.152).

The choice of genre supports a reading of the text as an illustration of suffering. The suburban gothic elements reveal the unsettling and sometimes grotesque realities of ordinary life, which, in blending with the domestic settings of the neodomestic drama, specifically locate such disquiet within the realms of women's experience. The gothic preoccupation with secrets and transgression, and its historical victimisation of women, further substantiates a reading of the collection as a litany of female misery and places it within a lengthy historical tradition.

Interpretation 2: The stories in *Bad Dreams* suggest that knowledge gained through experience is empowering.

While each story in this collection addresses often disturbing experiences, nevertheless there is an overriding sense of the strength and resilience displayed by each character. The characters are not unscathed by their experiences, but the ability to persist in the face of adversity or disappointment is a common theme. For example, Jane ('An Abduction') compartmentalises the pain of her experience with Daniel and raises a family of her own, and Claire in 'Flight' similarly puts aside her disappointment at being unable to reconcile with her sister. Greta ('Under the Sign of the Moon') also demonstrates persistence, despite two unfulfilling marriages and a significant illness.

Marina ('The Stain') also demonstrates a strength of character when she resists the actions of the old man and does not back down when his daughter Wendy accuses her of 'scheming behind her back' (p.43). Instead, she calls them out, Wendy 'recoil[ing] at her bluntness' (p.43) and even refuses the offer of financial compensation following the old man's death. For Marina, her self-respect is worth more than money.

In some stories the characters even seem to thrive as a result of their challenges. Ruby ('Her Share of Sorrow') persists in completing her novel despite being shamed by her family and feels 'writerly triumph' (p.194) on its completion, while Laura in 'Experience' finds a renewed sense of self-possession after the initial pain of Julian's rejection. Some of the younger characters, such as the little girl in 'Bad Dreams' or Sally in 'Silk Brocade', also illustrate strength in resisting the kinds of gendered social conventions that have defined some of their mothers' experiences. The little girl, for example, finds gratification in disrupting the 'world of her home' (p.120), overturning the static furniture she sees as symbolic of the future mapped out for her. These characters suggest that central to female identity is an ability to endure and even prevail in a world that seems at times set against them on the sole basis of their gender.

The collection supports this notion through genre choices; narrative structure; and the use of imagery and symbolism. Examples of the kinds of textual evidence you might use to support this reading include the following.

Genre choices

- The neodomestic drama, set within spaces traditionally associated with women, draws attention to how the roles of wife and mother can be both stifling and fulfilling ('One Saturday Morning', 'Flight').
- The suburban gothic genre seeks to reveal unsettling truths that exist behind the banal facade of suburbia. The often-idealised image of domestic bliss is subverted, most notably in 'Bad Dreams' with the normality of the concluding breakfast scene undermined by the reader's knowledge of the night-time disarray and the secrets kept by both mother and daughter.

Narrative structure

- The ambiguity of many of the stories' resolutions allows for varying interpretations – for example, Jane has crafted a life for herself yet she has always carried her disappointment ('An Abduction').
- Several stories conclude with the central character claiming agency, self-respect or pride: Marina in 'The Stain', for example, or Ruby in 'Her Share of Sorrow'. The wife in 'Bad Dreams' also faces her marriage with a new clarity and determination, even though readers might see her situation as tragic.

Imagery and symbolism

- Observation is a motif throughout the collection. Many characters are depicted observing others (Jane watching Fiona in 'An Abduction', Carrie observing her mother with Dom in 'One Saturday Morning', Claire's observation of her family in 'Flight'), or objects that represent others' lives (Hana's wardrobe in 'Experience', the dressing table miscellany in 'One Saturday Morning', the novels in 'Her Share of Sorrow), typically in order to learn from them.
- Symbols frequently point to the shattering of innocence or ignorance, as with the dead creature Marina once stumbled across in 'The Stain' or the deaths of fictional characters in both 'Bad Dreams' and 'Her Share of Sorrow'.

QUESTIONS & ANSWERS

This section focuses on your own analytical writing on the text, and gives you strategies for producing high-quality responses in your coursework and exam essays.

Essay writing – an overview

An essay on a literary work is a formal and serious piece of writing that presents your point of view on the text, usually in response to a given topic. Your 'point of view' in an essay is your interpretation of the meaning of the text's language, structure, characters, situations and events, supported by detailed analysis of textual evidence.

Analyse – don't summarise

In your essays it is important to avoid simply summarising what happens in a text.

- A **summary** is a description or paraphrase (retelling in different words) of the characters and events. For example: 'Macbeth has a horrifying vision of a dagger dripping with blood before he goes to murder King Duncan.'
- An **analysis** is an explanation of the real meaning or significance that lies 'beneath' the text's words (and images, for a film). For example: 'Macbeth's vision of a bloody dagger shows how deeply uneasy he is about the violent act he is contemplating, and conveys his sense that supernatural forces are impelling him to act.'

A limited amount of summary is sometimes necessary to let your reader know which part of the text you wish to discuss. However, always keep this to a minimum and follow it immediately with your analysis of what this part of the text is really telling us.

Plan your essay

Carefully plan your essay so that you have a clear idea of what you are going to say. The plan ensures that your ideas flow logically, that your argument remains consistent and that you stay on the topic. An essay plan should be a list of **brief dot points** covering no more than half a page.

- Include your central argument or main contention – a concise statement of your overall response to the topic.
- Write three or four dot points for each paragraph, indicating the main idea and evidence/examples from the text. Note that in your essay you will need to *expand* on these points and *analyse* the evidence.

Structure your essay

An essay is a complete, self-contained piece of writing. It has a clear beginning (the introduction), middle (several body paragraphs) and end (the last paragraph or conclusion). It must also have a central argument that runs throughout, linking each paragraph to form a coherent whole. See examples of introductions and conclusions in the 'Analysing a sample topic' and 'Sample answer' sections.

The introduction establishes your overall response to the topic. It includes your main contention and outlines the main evidence you will refer to in the course of the essay. Write your introduction *after* you have done a plan and *before* you write the rest of the essay.

The body paragraphs argue your case – they present evidence from the text and explain how this evidence supports your argument. Each body paragraph needs:

- a strong **topic sentence** (usually the first sentence) that states the main point being made in the paragraph
- **evidence** from the text, including some brief quotations
- **analysis** of the textual evidence, with **explanation** of its significance and how it supports your argument
- **links back to the topic** in one or more statements, usually towards the end of the paragraph.

Connect the body paragraphs so that your discussion flows smoothly. Use some linking words and phrases such as 'similarly' and 'on the other hand', though don't start every paragraph like this. Another strategy is to use a significant word from the last sentence of one paragraph in the first sentence of the next.

Use key terms from the topic – or synonyms for them – throughout, so the relevance of your discussion to the topic is always clear.

The conclusion ties everything together and finishes the essay. It includes strong statements that emphasise your central argument and provide a clear response to the topic.

Avoid simply restating the points made earlier in the essay – this will end on a very flat note and imply that you have run out of ideas and vocabulary. The conclusion should be a logical extension of what you have written, not just a repetition or summary of it. Writing an effective conclusion can be a challenge. Try using these tips:

- Start by linking back to the final sentence of the second-last paragraph, rather than leaping to your main contention straight away – this helps your writing to flow.
- Use synonyms and expressions with equivalent meanings to vary your vocabulary. This allows you to reinforce your line of argument without being repetitive.
- When planning your essay, think of one or two broad statements or observations about the text's wider meaning. These should be related to the topic and your overall argument. Keep them for the conclusion, since they will give you something 'new' to say but still follow logically from your discussion. The introduction will be focused on the topic, but the conclusion can present a wider view of the text.

Essay topics

1. Discuss how Tessa Hadley uses the perspective of the outsider to communicate her themes.
2. 'Tessa Hadley's stories suggest that experience comes at a cost.' Discuss.
3. 'In these stories, fear and desire are in constant tension.' Discuss.
4. Discuss the role of symbolism in drawing attention to key themes in *Bad Dreams*.
5. 'The experiences of the characters within *Bad Dreams* are unique to women.' To what extent do you agree?
6. 'A key value demonstrated by Hadley's characters is perseverance.' Discuss.
7. 'Hadley's stories explore the tension between conforming and transgression.' Discuss.
8. "She couldn't get rid of the terrible knowledge that Dom had brought; it seemed to be stuck inside her, in her stomach or her throat." How does Hadley show that knowledge is central to personal growth?
9. 'Tessa Hadley's stories are quietly subversive.' To what extent do you agree?
10. 'Many stories in *Bad Dreams* chart the transition from innocence to experience'. Discuss.

Analysing a sample topic

'Tessa Hadley frequently illustrates the significance of everyday experience.' Discuss.

First look at any instruction words in the topic. Here you are directed to discuss – that is, to explore the topic, considering it from different angles, supported by examples from the text. Next identify and define key terms relating to the text: here, 'illustrates' (which tells you to explain how textual evidence supports the topic) and 'significance of everyday experience' (this points you to the thematic areas you will be exploring).

Pay close attention to words like 'never' or 'frequently' in a topic, as these will shape your response; you might explore a 'partially agree' answer, since you may consider that some stories do not engage with the 'everyday'. However, given that the majority of the stories in this text do draw attention to the impacts of seemingly ordinary experiences, you may find greater evidence to agree with the topic than to challenge it.

Another step in analysing the topic is to reflect on the individual key words. A stronger line of argument will clearly outline the parameters by which you define each term. For example, consider meanings of 'significance', such as 'importance' or 'consequence'; also consider for whom these experiences are significant. Events and experiences do not necessarily need to have a large or widespread effect for them to be considered significant. Similarly, consider the implications of 'everyday experience'.

You also need to frame a clear contention (central response to the topic). For the topic above, this might be 'the text shows that everyday experiences can have significance, even if only for the individual'. Another possibility is 'the text draws attention to the significance of women's everyday experiences, which are often overlooked'. You might even engage with gender politics and consider how women's experiences, particularly within the domestic spaces represented in this collection, are often dismissed as insignificant. The first contention forms the basis of the following sample response paragraphs and notes.

Sample introduction

> Representations of the mundane and commonplace are central to many stories in Tessa Hadley's collection *Bad Dreams*. Experiences range from childhood nightmares, sibling conflicts, the breakdown of relationships or visits from family friends, to the less mundane, but equally

commonplace. Despite the everyday nature of these events, they can carry great significance in shaping the course of an individual's life – for better or worse.

Body paragraph outline

Paragraph 1: Identify examples of everyday experiences and how they might be considered significant. You might group these by type, such as:

- childhood experiences ('One Saturday Morning', 'Bad Dreams', 'Her Share of Sorrow')
- domestic experiences ('The Stain', 'One Saturday Morning', 'Flight')
- sexual experiences ('An Abduction', 'Experience', 'Silk Brocade').

Paragraph 2: Identify a key example of a seemingly mundane experience that brings about a sudden flash of insight for the character.

- In 'The Stain', Anthony's revelation of his grandfather's history in the South African Defence Force causes Marina to reassess her relationship as carer for the old man.
- In 'Her Share of Sorrow', Ruby's simple act of reading her first adult novel is revelatory; she was previously unaware that 'books could transport [her] like this' (p.188).
- The unnamed girl in 'Bad Dreams' is troubled by the nightmare ending to *Swallows and Amazons* that reveals to her the realities of female experience: the transgressive pirate girl is punished with death while the maternal Susan lives 'to a ripe old age' (p.116). As a result, she is troubled by an awareness of her parents' lives and feels 'a sudden passion … to disrupt this world of her home' (p.120) by upturning the furniture.

Paragraph 3: Choose a key example of commonplace experience having long-reaching implications.

- Jane's rejection by Daniel in 'An Abduction', as well as her awareness of 'the justice of her defeat' (p.17) at the hands of the more worldly and conventionally attractive Fiona, is suggested to have shaped her more conventional life choices. Hadley's use of prolepsis and the sudden shift in perspective at the end of the story force the reader to recognise how she has carried the experience 'in a sealed compartment' (p.27) throughout her life.

- Laura's attempt to seduce Julian in 'Experience' represents experimentation after the conventionality (or even banality, given its description) of her marriage. Despite Julian's polite rejection, the story's ending reveals that Laura nonetheless finds herself infused with a new-found confidence and worldliness, as if she had been 'initiated into something after all' (p.110).

Sample conclusion

> Many of the characters in *Bad Dreams* find themselves in situations that might be considered 'everyday' or even mundane. Nevertheless, these experiences are shown to be significantly formative, shaping identities or facilitating transitions from innocence to experience. Often characters carry these experiences throughout their lives (revealed through Hadley's proleptic transitions in time), and their significance is underscored through the use of potent symbolism. The collection encourages readers to reconsider the seemingly banal, as the everyday experiences of these women and girls are shown to have genuine significance.

SAMPLE ANSWER

'In *Bad Dreams*, characters seem to be "pushing across the threshold of safety into a thrilling unknown".' To what extent do you agree?

Characters in Tessa Hadley's *Bad Dreams* are frequently depicted as transitioning from a place of naivety or innocence into a world replete with adult knowledge. These characters desire experience that, through age or ignorance, they have been denied. In some cases, crossing the threshold results in personal growth and a greater sense of confidence, while in others the characters suffer as a result of the perspicacity they acquire. Thus, the collection depicts this moment of transformation as alluring but not without consequence.

Several of the collection's characters are young girls on the cusp of adolescence, seeking to leave behind the relative safety of childhood and enter the adult world. 'An Abduction' is the clearest example of this, as Jane finds herself frustrated at not being 'more thoroughly embarked on her teenage self', and when the opportunity arises to accompany a group of boys for a transgressive afternoon, she seizes it in order to take 'the fated trek towards adulthood'. Adult women, too, yearn for experience outside of the conventions dictated by society. Edith in 'Deeds Not Words', for example, finds her affair with Fitzsimmon revelatory, having 'dreaded that [her] body would bloom and fade under her clothes without any man ever knowing it', while Greta in 'Under the Sign of the Moon' seeks out the company of Mitchell despite being uncertain of his intentions. In these stories, female characters are attracted by the thrilling unknown of sensual experience.

Sometimes this pursuit of experience brings rewards. In 'Experience', Laura's rite of passage results in a new-found sense of self-possession. Unsettled following the breakdown of her marriage, she is initially intimidated by Hana's overt sensuality and confidence, yet 'powerfully impressed' by her glamorous lifestyle, represented by the distinctive furnishings, luscious wardrobe and refrigerator stocked with spicy foods Laura had 'never tasted before'. Despite being married for six years, she feels 'inexperienced', her own life mundane in contrast, particularly after discovering Hana's diaries detailing her affair with Julian. Deciding she no longer wants to 'view things coldly, from outside', Laura wears Hana's clothes and attempts to seduce Julian, her physical hunger in this scene symbolic of her yearning for experience. Although Julian rejects her advances, Laura nonetheless finds herself transformed, as people 'take [her] more seriously' and regard her as 'older and more experienced'. The knowledge she has gained is not from adopting Hana's life but from realising the value in her own experiences, symbolised in her changing back into her own clothes and 'hunt[ing] out [her] box of souvenirs', totems of her own life that she finds suddenly 'consoling'. The first-person point of view encourages readers to accept Laura's conclusion that she has 'been initiated into something after all', and celebrate the fact that she is able to overcome her ennui and take control of her life.

In other stories, the characters are punished for crossing the threshold. Edith, for example, is left distraught when Fitzsimmon ends their affair, knowing that she has 'forfeited the white flower of a blameless life', while Ruby ('Her Share of Sorrow') is mortified when her family laugh at her novel. Greta, feeling her illness bars her from 'the world of sexual attraction', nevertheless decides to accept the much younger Mitchell's invitation to meet him at the Palm House. She dreams it is a 'crazily dilapidated' glasshouse, with a 'solid mass of plant growth pressed against the steamed-up glass', a symbol of her own repressed desires struggling against a body she regards as defective. Mitchell represents transgressive possibility, much like Ian, her unconventional first husband, for whom she still 'yearned, treacherously'. When Mitchell knocks a drink over her and unexpectedly places his head into her lap, however, Greta is left 'burning with humiliation' at the 'spectacle'. In ending her stories with women feeling shamed, Hadley directs our attention to the tragedy of women being chastened for seeking experience outside the boundaries dictated by convention.

For some characters, however, the unknown is not necessarily thrilling, but is instead disconcerting. In 'One Saturday Morning', Carrie struggles with Dom's revelation of his wife's death, the 'terrible knowledge' of which becomes 'stuck inside her'. Despite feeling sorrow, her reaction is driven by something 'selfish and self-protective', her innocent world view tainted with the intrusion of adult grief. Carrie longs for Dom to leave and 'the whole ordinary process of living to start into motion again'. When she later witnesses Dom's grief-stricken pass at her mother, she feels even more 'disembodied', aware that some complex adult interaction beyond her comprehension is taking place. When Carrie snuggles with her mother in the final scene of the story, she starts to wonder whether she imagined the incident, a worrying vision of adult behaviour as yet 'unavailable to children'. Presented through the eyes of a ten-year-old, this moment reminds us how precarious childhood innocence really is, and like the insect that lands on Paul's book, the intrusion of the adult world can be both fascinating and grotesque.

Bad Dreams contains many stories of characters crossing thresholds into worlds previously unknown to them. Several characters actively seek out new experiences, sometimes with unintended and unpleasant consequences, while others have these experiences unexpectedly thrust upon them. Throughout the collection, Hadley develops the theme that personal growth comes from experience; sometimes this growth arises from a greater understanding of oneself, or it may be an insight into the often unfair ways in which the world works. In presenting readers with a variety of outcomes – some empowering, some shaming – Hadley reveals the risks associated with seeking experience, but portrays these experiences as intrinsic to personal growth and development.

REFERENCES & READING

Text

Hadley, T 2017, *Bad Dreams and Other Stories*, Penguin Random House, UK.

References

Clark, A 2011, 'Tessa Hadley: A life in writing', *The Guardian*, 28 February, https://www.theguardian.com/books/2011/feb/28/tessa-hadley-life-writing-fiction

Cutaia, S 2017, '"Bad Dreams" finds magic in the everyday lives of women', *Chicago Review of Books*, 17 May, https://chireviewofbooks.com/2017/05/17/bad-dreams-tessa-hadley-review/

Hall, S & Hadley, T 2017, 'Sarah Hall and Tessa Hadley in conversation', *Granta*, 9 August, https://granta.com/sarah-hall-tessa-hadley-conversation/

Jarvis, C 2017, 'That's more like it: Tessa Hadley's "Bad Dreams and Other Stories"', *LA Review of Books*, 1 July, https://lareviewofbooks.org/article/thats-more-like-it-tessa-hadleys-bad-dreams-and-other-stories/

Niedenthal, A 2017, 'New routes in fiction: Tessa Hadley with Alec Niedenthal', *The Brooklyn Rail*, November, https://brooklynrail.org/2017/11/fiction/New-Routes-in-Fiction-tessa-hadley-with-alec-niedenthal

Orr, KJ 2017, 'Bad Dreams by Tessa Hadley review – enthralling short stories', *The Guardian*, 28 January, https://www.theguardian.com/books/2017/jan/28/bad-dreams-tessa-hadley-review

Smart, K 2020, 'Tessa Hadley: "There's nothing unpolitical about intimate stories of family life"', Curtis Brown Creative, 30 July, https://www.curtisbrowncreative.co.uk/blog/tessa-hadley-author-interview

Treisman, D 2013, 'This Week in Fiction: Tessa Hadley', *The New Yorker*, 13 September, https://www.newyorker.com/books/page-turner/this-week-in-fiction-tessa-hadley-4

Treisman, D 2014, 'This Week in Fiction: Tessa Hadley', *The New Yorker*, 18 August, https://www.newyorker.com/books/page-turner/week-fiction-tessa-hadley

Treisman, D 2015, 'This Week in Fiction: Tessa Hadley', *The New Yorker*, 20 July, https://www.newyorker.com/books/page-turner/fiction-this-week-tessa-hadley-2015-07-27

Other resources

Crown, S 2017, 'Too much experience', *TLS. Times Literary Supplement*, no. 5938, 20 January, *Gale Literature Resource Center*, https://go.gale.com/ps/i.do?id=GALE%7CA634849456&sid=googleScholar&v=2.1&it=r&linkaccess=abs&issn=0307661X&p=LitRC&sw=w&userGroupName=anon%7Ed815a1df

Hadley, T 2016, 'At home in the past', *The New Yorker*, 30 May, https://www.newyorker.com/magazine/2016/06/06/tessa-hadley-rereads-the-secret-garden

Hanson, C 2015, 'Fiction: From Realism to Postmodernism and beyond', in M Eagleton & E Parker (eds), *The History of British Women's Writing, 1970–Present*, vol. 10, pp.23–35, Springer, UK.

Kellaway, K 2022, 'Novelist Tessa Hadley: If I met my characters, I might not like them', *The Guardian*, 9 January, https://www.theguardian.com/books/2022/jan/08/tessa-hadley-free-love-interview